Pete **Shelley**

I don't want to classify you...

The design and intent of this significant book is minimalist, so I will be brief. It is an honour to publish the lyrics of Pete Shelley. Eyewear has a history of publishing song lyrics, considering them a form of literature, just as the Nobel committee now does as well. In particular, we have published poets-songwriters such as Paul Muldoon (winner of a Pulitzer prize), and Keaton Henson. Nothing could be more thrilling, however, than being the publisher of these seminal texts by a top British musician.

I consider 'Homosapien' to be one of the greatest songs ever written; it seems effortless in its capacity to instil the passion and angst of late Oscar Wilde. Indeed, many of the songs in this book are models of songcraft, for their economy, wit, surprise and clarity. It is possible to read this book, even without knowing the music that accompanies the words, and thoroughly enjoy the work. One of the great delights, of course, is being able to go back and listen again to favourites, and new discoveries, with the book in hand, for this is a record of a truly remarkable career.

Dr Todd Swift
Director Eyewear Publishing Ltd
Poet-in-residence (Visiting Scholar)
Cambridge University, Pembroke College
October 1 2017 – September 30 2018

Fluttering Hearts

When invited to write this introduction my initial thought was that I could tackle it either historically or emotionally. Both approaches are equally valid as Buzzcocks have shaped both my history and my natural emotions. Suffice to say, Pete Shelley's lyrics were to form a vivid soundtrack to my life and my career, and forty years have done nothing at all to dim their potency and emotional thrust.

History

Meeting Pete Shelley in April 1977, just a week before I was to see him perform with Buzzcocks for the first time, was a major turning point for me. He had come to a party that I had thrown with my friend from art school, John McGeoch, at the flat where we lived on Wilmslow Road in Rusholme, Manchester. He arrived with Buzzcocks' former singer Howard Devoto, their manager Richard Boon, and my college friend Linder. She had already given me Buzzcocks' seminal EP, 'Spiral Scratch', having secured an advance copy for me several weeks previously. This meeting proved to be pivotal for us all.

Richard asked me to design a poster to advertise gigs. I designed and printed the poster in college and it featured the Buzzcocks logo which is still in use today. I went on to work with Linder to create artwork for their first United Artists single 'Orgasm Addict' and set about defining an approach to music packaging which we intended to be as fresh as the Sex Pistols' graphics as it was distinctive from them.

Working with Richard, Pete and the rest of the band over subsequent years, we established a knowingly sophisticated, yet often disarmingly simple graphic style that fully complemented Pete's lyrics.

Emotion

From the first moment 'Spiral Scratch' blasted out of my record player I instinctively realised that Buzzcocks would have an incredible and indelible effect on me and on the creative direction my design work was about to take. The songs were exciting and motivational, the lyrics had a visceral edge, and crucially they fed my imagination and evoked all kinds of visual imagery in my mind.

I was to do all of my growing up as a designer with Pete Shelley and Buzzcocks. I had gone to art school looking for some real purpose for creative endeavour and specifically had a desire to use graphics and typography to express more than bland promotion. Graphic design was about language and emotion, and about how typography colours what we read, hear and understand. The designer's role is to convey implicitly that emotion, as quickly and effectively as possible. Pete's lyrics, driven as they are by honesty and passion, and stripped of excessive linguistic detail, both delighted me and repeatedly challenged me to match their simplicity and purity.

For me 'What Do I Get?' stands alongside John Lennon's 'Help!' as the all-time classic love song. It is a song that encapsulates a certain forlorn angst yet, with its harmonies, still sounds like a joyously romantic plea. This was only my second sleeve for Buzzcocks, and distilled to its essence, representing the tone of the two songs on the record in colour alone, it is perhaps the closest in spirit to a Shelley lyric that I have managed. Maybe I was also subconsciously referencing those early Beatles records on the Parlophone label by choosing green as the principal colour.

Of all of Pete's songs of love, lust and loss, 'I Believe' is arguably the greatest. I was eternally rewarded when the lyric "triangular cover concealing another aspect from view" reflected the sleeve design I had shown him during the recording. I still don't know whether its inclusion was by design or caught in the web of fate, but I believe that my confrontationally complex design was an accurate representation of his alliterative lyrical challenge to life, its complexities and its contradictions.

I'll leave it there. I'll be leaving, but I do believe in, Pete Shelley.

Malcolm Garrett

Lyrics

A Different Kind Of Tension

Wait here
Come in
Be yourself
Obey the law

Go there
Stay out
Be someone else
Break the law

Be ambitious
Plan ahead
Decide for yourself
Save money

Be modest
Be spontaneous
Listen to others
Spend money

Be good
Be wise
Be safe
Be satisfied
Be honest
Be faithful
Be sane
Be strong
Be enigmatic
Be aggressive
Be brave
Be humane
Be critical
Be temperamental
Be sad
Be normal

Be evil
Be foolish
Be dangerous
Be envious
Be deceitful
Be perfidious
Be mad
Be weak
Be plain
Be peaceful
Be timid
Be cruel
Be appreciative
Calm
Be happy
Be unusual

Stop
Live
Yes
Rebel
Right
Sit down
Create
Accept
Talk

Go
Die
No
Submit
Wrong
Stand up
Destroy
Reject
Silence

Speed up	Slow down
This way	That way
Right	Left
Present	Absent
Open	Closed
Entrance	Exit
Believe	Doubt
Truth	Lies
Escape	Meet
Love	Hate
Thank you	Flunk
Clarify	Pollute
Simple	Complex
Nothing	Something
Stop	Go
Live	Die
Yes	No
Rebel	Submit
Right	Wrong
Sit down	Stand up
Create	Destroy
Accept	Reject
Talk	Silence

All Over You

I'm a poor man deep in my pocket
But in my heart I'm a millionaire
But a perfect sense of direction
Ain't no use if you're going nowhere

You're like a wacky man's walk on
And you think I have eccentric ideas
Better latent than never
Just that thought kept me warm through your fears

When you kiss do you keep your eyes open?
I'd love to linger on the taste of your tongue
Would our souls be in imminent danger?
I can't see how what we do could be wrong

A sandwich short of a picnic
Trying hard to save the wages of sin
It helps if you think quick
When the razor feels soft to your skin

I wanna be all over all over you
I wanna be all over all over you

Looking for love let me make you an offer
That's as tender as a tender can be
Give me a ring or just drop me a postcard
And turn my fantasy to reality

A nasty stain on the carpet
Perfectly matches all the ones in your bed
Instead of grinding your gusset
Why not give me the pleasure instead?

I wanna be all over all over you
I wanna be all over all over you

I wanna be all over all over you
I wanna be all over all over you

A nasty stain on the carpet
Perfectly matches all the ones in my bed
Instead of grinding your gusset
Why not give me the pleasure instead?

I wanna be all over all over you
I wanna be all over all over you

There's one more thing I just gotta say
The very thought of which drives me insane
You keep saying that we're over again and again and again
I guess I'd better be resigned that you've made up your mind
And if you never wanna see me again

I wanna be all over all over you
I wanna be all over all over you
I wanna be all over all over you
I wanna be all over all over you
I wanna be all over all over you
I wanna be all over all over you
I wanna be all over all over you
I wanna be all over all over you

Are Everything

Your looks
My charm
My own imagination
My loves
Your hates
Your own infatuation
Are everything
Are everything

My hopes
Your fears
Your only limitation
Your thoughts
My schemes
My own evaluation
Are everything
Are everything

My looks
Your charm
Your own imagination
Your loves
My hates
My own infatuation
Are everything
Are everything

Your hopes
My fears
My only limitation
My thoughts
Your schemes
Your own evaluation
Are everything
Are everything

Blue Eyes

My aches are all aching
Opportunities taken
I'll be alright in a minute
It's funny though innit
The way that it happens?

Sick and tired of this love thing
Like I'm tired of everything
I'll be alright in a minute
It's funny though innit
The way that it happens?
I'll be alright in a minute
It's funny though innit
The way that it happens?

Blue eyes blue eyes
I tried to teach you everything
Blue eyes blue eyes
You thought you could do anything

Your ideas of pleasure
Are best taken at leisure
I'll be alright in a minute
It's funny though innit
The way it all happens?

I've this deep-felt suspicion
For your so-called tradition
I'll be alright in a minute
It's funny though innit
The way that it happens?
I'll be alright in a minute
It's funny though innit
The way it all happens?

Blue eyes blue eyes
You said I could do anything
But you've gone too far
Blue eyes blue eyes
You thought you would do everything
But you've gone too far

The loneliest sound I've ever heard
Was the slamming of the door
I don't know whose side you think you're on
But you make love like a tug of war

Sick and tired of this love thing
Like I'm tired of everything
I'll be alright in a minute
It's funny though innit
The way that it happens?
I'll be alright in a minute
It's funny though innit
The way it all happens?

Blue eyes blue eyes
I thought I'd show you everything
But you've gone too far
Blue eyes blue eyes
You wouldn't show me anything
But you've gone too far
Blue eyes blue eyes
I thought we could be anything
But you've gone too far
Blue eyes truth lies
At the centre of everything
But you've gone too far
But you've gone too far
But you've gone too far
But you've gone too far

Choices

Choices

Indecision just can't make up my mind
Is there a solution anyway?
I thought you were the only one
Who could take me there

Choices, choices, choices

All at once I realise the reasons why
Therefore the only one is you
You said I was the only one
Who could take you there

Choices, choices, choices

Releasing the energy that makes me want
To shout out loud when you're not there
You said I was the only one
Who could take you there

Choices, choices, choices

In between what I have seen and what I dream
I hope that I will find you there
You said I'm not the only one
Who could take you there

Choices, choices, choices

Indecision just can't make up your mind
Is there a solution anyway?
You said I'm not the only one
Who could take you there

Choices, choices, choices

In between what I have seen and what I dream
I hope that I will find you there
I guess I'm not the only one
Who can take you there

Choices, choices, choices

Choices, choices, choices

Credit

Paradise is a platinum card
Behind the wheel of your car
With a new pair of trainers
Designer clothes
Go on, I'll have seven of those
And go to ski where it snows
Its bounty sustains us

Credit
In love with the never-never
Wish I could get something I really need

Videophones
With all the latest ringtones
You buy-to-let your new home
Don't care what you're spending
Then just like that
Reminders under the mat
Of your flat full of tat
The pile of debts never ending

Credit
In love with the never-never
Wish I could get something I really need

Credit
Saddled with debt for ever
Wish I could get something I really need

Credit
In love with the never-never
How I wish I had something I really need

Crystal Night

I read the news, you saw the headlines
I know your secret, do you know mine?
Somebody said they're getting closer
I guess we don't have all that much time

They're lighting bonfires in the distance
You know some things in life will never change
So please don't say there was no warning
Just hold on tight it's crystal night again
It's crystal night again

This lot won't stop with just your records
This lot won't stop with all your dirty books
This lot won't stop don't need excuses
Don't like your lifestyle don't like your looks

They're lighting bonfires in the distance
You know some things in life will never change
But please don't say there was no warning
Just hold on tight it's crystal night again
It's crystal night again

I read the news, you're in the headlines
You've sold your secret, will you tell mine?
I hear a shout they're getting closer
I guess we don't have all that much time

This lot won't stop with just your records
This lot won't stop with all your dirty books
This lot won't stop don't need excuses
Don't like your lifestyle don't like your looks
So please don't say there was no warning
Just hold on tight it's crystal night again
It's crystal night again

Disappointment

It's said history repeats itself
Well that is nothing new
But somewhere in the scheme of things
There lurks an awful truth

All the disappointment of the world
All the disappointment of the world

Life is a strict teacher
Whose lessons must be learned
And optimists turn pessimists
After experience

All the disappointment of the world
All the disappointment of the world

Try to understand
No matter what you plan
You'll never get what you demand

All the disappointment of the world
All the disappointment of the world

Try to understand
No matter what you plan
You'll never get what you demand

Betwixt and between
Nightmare and dream
It's really as bad as it seems

All the disappointment of the world
All the disappointment of the world

Do Anything

What I know I can't say
No one's asking questions anyway
Sometimes I feel so outta touch
I hope you know that you mean so much
It seems so simple to be so true
You'll do anything when you have to
You'll do anything when you have to

Don't need money for what I got in mind
You can only spend it while you're wasting time
I had a dream the other day
That made the darkness roll away
Of all I know I guess this much is true
You'll do anything when you have to
You'll do anything when you have to

The fight we had in the middle of the night
When I walked out the door
Was I forsaken?
Wouldn't you love me any more?
Am I mistaken?
Had I imagined every wrong?
I hope that I get back before too long

I wish everybody could be like me
But if we're all the same where would variety be?
I'm only after the peace of mind
Of a good friend that's so hard to find
Would I give it all away just to be with you?
You'll do anything when you have to
You'll do anything when you have to

The fight we had in the middle of the night
When I walked out the door
Was I forsaken?
Would you love me any more?

Am I mistaken?
Have I imagined every wrong?
I hope that I get back before too long

Of all I know I guess this much is true
You'll do anything when you have to
You'll do anything when you have to

Do It

Here again
Playing the lonely game
Blind as a fool who won't see
Suddenly
Taking control again
What could be happening to me?

My only consolation
Is that someday you'll care
My source of inspiration
You don't get far
When you're going nowhere

I can do it, do it, do it
Till the morning comes
Like the river fills the sea
I can do it, do it, do it
Like incessant drums
I can do it like the birds and the bees

Hesitate
Is there no end to it?
So tired of living a lie
Time won't wait
Too late to start again
Wander while wondering why

My only consolation
Is that someday you'll care
Perverse sophistication
You won't get far
If you're going nowhere

I can do it, do it, do it
Till the morning comes

Like the river fills the sea
I can do it, do it, do it
Like incessant drums
I can do it like the birds and the bees

I can do it, do it, do it
Till the morning comes
Like the river fills the sea
I can do it, do it, do it
Like incessant drums
I can do it like the birds and the bees

My only consolation
Is that someday you'll care
My source of inspiration
You don't get far
If you're going nowhere

It's not infatuation
To hope that you're the one to care
My final consolation
You won't get far
You're going nowhere

I can do it, do it, do it
Till the morning comes
Like the river fills the sea
I can do it, do it, do it
Like incessant drums
I can do it like the birds and the bees
I can do it, do it, do it
Till the morning comes
I can do it, do it, do it, do it

Dreamin'

Dreamin'
Am I dreamin'?
Try as hard as I can
I just can't get you out of my mind
Dreamin'
Am I dreamin'?
Will my dreams come true
Or am I simply wasting my time?

Well, I told you that I'm sorry
Didn't mean to make you cry
But look at it from my point of view
It's the little things in life
On which our happiness depends
And what's the use if any
In trying to survive
All the problems that the world can provide
If at the end of all of this
We haven't got the time to be friends?

Dreamin'
Am I dreamin'?
Try as hard as I can
I just can't get you out of my mind
Dreamin'
I must be dreamin'?
Will my dreams come true
Or am I simply wasting my time?

Well, I get this funny feeling
That just won't stay away
You know it drives me almost out of my mind
It seems that life's too short
For us to carry on the way that we do
Too much discrimination

Is keeping us apart
And I don't think I can take any more
I only hope and pray
I can find a way to say
'I love you'

Oh, wouldn't it be great
If we could be in that state
For ever
Just a moment with you
In the next year or two
Or whenever
Let's make history together

Dreamin'
Am I dreamin'?
Try as hard as I can
I just can't get you out of my mind
Dreamin'
I must be dreamin'?
Will my dreams come true
Or am I simply wasting my time?
Try as hard as I can
I just can't get you out of my mind
I just can't get you out of my mind

ESP

Do you believe in ESP?
I do and I'm tryna get through to you
If you're picking up off me
Then you know just what to do
Think

Brainwaves transmitted from my mind
Of a magnetic kind
I don't know what to do
If I can't get through to you
So think

Do you believe in ESP?
I've been tryna get through to you
If you've been picking up off me
Then you'll know just what to do
Don't you?

Ever Fallen In Love
(With Someone You Shouldn't've Have)

You spurn my natural emotions
You make me feel I'm dirt
And I'm hurt
And if I start a commotion
I run the risk of losing you
And that's worse

Ever fallen in love
With someone
Ever fallen in love
In love with someone
Ever fallen in love
In love with someone
You shouldn't've fallen in love with?

I can't see much of a future
Unless we find out what's to blame
What a shame
And we won't be together much longer
Unless we realise that we are the same

Ever fallen in love
With someone
Ever fallen in love
In love with someone
Ever fallen in love
In love with someone
You shouldn't've fallen in love with?

You disturb my natural emotions
You make me feel I'm dirt
And I'm hurt
And if I start a commotion
I'll only end up losing you
And that's worse

Ever fallen in love
With someone
Ever fallen in love
In love with someone
Ever fallen in love
In love with someone
You shouldn't've fallen in love with?

Ever fallen in love
With someone
Ever fallen in love
In love with someone
Ever fallen in love
In love with someone
You shouldn't've fallen in love with?

Ever fallen in love
With someone
Ever fallen in love
In love with someone
Ever fallen in love
In love with someone
You shouldn't've fallen in love with?
Fallen in love with
Ever fallen in love with someone
You shouldn't've fallen in love with?

Everybody's Happy Nowadays

I was so tired of being upset
Always wanting something I never could get
Life's an illusion
Love is a dream
But I don't know what it is

Everybody's happy nowadays
Everybody's happy nowadays

I was so tired of being upset
Always wanting something I never could get
Life's an illusion
Love is a dream
But I don't know what it is 'cos

Everybody's happy nowadays
Everybody's happy nowadays

Life's an illusion
Love is the dream
But I don't know what it is
Everyone's saying things to me
But I know it's okay, okay

Everybody's happy nowadays
Everybody's happy nowadays

Everybody's happy nowadays
Everybody's happy nowadays

Life's an illusion
Love is a dream
Life's an illusion
Love is the dream
Life's the illusion
Love is a dream
Life's the illusion
Love is the dream

Everybody's happy nowadays
Everybody's happy nowadays
Todays are good

Bet you are tired of being upset
Always wanting something you never can get
Life's no illusion
Love's not a dream
Now I know just what it is

Everybody's happy nowadays
Everybody's happy nowadays

Fiction Romance

A fiction romance
I love this love story
That never seems to happen in my life
A fiction romance
All love and glory
That never seems to happen in my life

Dreams of love and dreams of pain
And dreams again, again, again
A gain which can be yours just by taking hold
Dreams that I can realise
Are quite contained within your eyes
Say fiction romance is not so old

A fiction romance
The love of the ages
That never seems to matter in my life
A fiction romance
On magazine pages
That never seems to feature in my life

Dreaming scheming unaware
That quite somewhere some unaware folk
Are not thinking 'bout what they have been told
Something strange is happening to
The way I see the world I view
That fiction romance is not sold

As a fiction romantic
I never expected
All these things to happen in real life
And no fiction romantic
Could ever've predicted
All the things that happen in my life

When I don't know what to do
I just think about me and you
If I was a little stronger then I'd be bold
Something strange is happening to me
I don't know what these shivers mean to you
Is this a fiction and a romance getting hold?

A fiction romance

Flat-Pack Philosophy

I'm cracking up
Can't take the strain
From Heaven to Hell
And back again

And so each night
I say a prayer
Someone to love
Someone to care

Hold on
Why am I here?
What are we living for?
All of my hopes, dreams and desires
Assembly required
That's flat-pack philosophy

So when my thoughts
Make me depressed
I think the best
And fuck the rest

Despite it all
The future's key
The double decker bus
The one I didn't see

Hold on
Why am I here?
What are we living for?
All of my hopes, dreams and desires
Assembly required
That's flat-pack philosophy

Hold on
Why am I here?
What are we living for?
All of my hopes, dreams and desires
Assembly required
That's flat-pack philosophy

Flat-pack philosophy
Flat-pack philosophy

Friends

Well, I've been up all night
Couldn't get to dream at all
Trying hard not to make a decision
You know it doesn't seem right
When your back's to the wall
To be accused of sensationalism
But the way things are going
Wouldn't be at all surprised
If a song I like won the next Eurovision

I turn around and it all looks the same
I don't even know if I'll ever be loved again
The only thing I can rely on is change

It's a mixed up world
These are mixed up times
And the recipe of life's mixed up too
But if it's the quality of ingredients that matter
I would award myself a cordon bleu
But I can't help thinking
That you wouldn't understand
Unless I did a lot of explaining to you

I look around but it still looks the same
I don't even know if I'll ever be loved again
The only thing I can rely on is change

You know I have often wondered
If what you're telling me's true?
But I know that I can make it
If I have my friends to see me through

I look around but it still looks the same
I don't even know if I'll ever be loved again
The only thing I can rely on is change

You know I have often wondered
If what you're telling me's true?
But I know that I can make it
If I have my friends to see me through

It's a mixed up world
These are mixed up times
And the recipe of life's mixed up too
But if it's the quality of ingredients that matter
I would award myself a cordon bleu
But I can't help thinking
That you wouldn't understand
Unless I did a lot of explaining to you

I look around but it still looks the same
I don't even know if I'll ever be loved again
The only thing I can rely on is change

I look around but it still looks the same
I don't even know if I'll ever be loved again
The only thing I can rely on is change

Get On Our Own

Honey, I saw you yesterday
On my way home
Baby, I craved for you today
So I decided to phone
So why don't we get together soon
And er, get on our own?
Just think of what me and you could do
If we get on our own
If we could get on our own
If we could get on our own

Honey, I saw you again today
And I er, liked what I saw
So why don't we meet tonight
Then I could er, see a bit more?
So how's about we get together soon
Well, why be alone?
Just think of what me and you could do
If we get on our own
If we could get on our own
If we could get on our own

Just think of it
Me and you
Us together
Yes, just we two
Think of all the things
That me and you could do
If we get on our own
If we could get on our own
If we could get on our own
Just me and you

Aw

Give It To Me

When I look into your eyes
I can see the fire of desire reflect to me
Give me your love
Give it to me
Give it to me

Holding me the way you do
I just can't deny that you feel the same way too
Give me your love
Give it to me
Give it to me

Don't you know that I care about you
But I just can't wait?
Give it
Give it to me

When you're lying next to me
I just get the urge to consummate ecstasy
Give me your love
Give it to me
Give it to me

Holding me the way you do
I just can't deny that you feel the same way too
Give me your love
Give it to me
Give it to me

Don't you know that I care about you
But I just can't wait?
Give it
Give it to me

Look at me while I tell you 'bout love
Don't you know that you should never doubt love?

With you near I feel you warm inside
When it comes to the real thing there's no compromise
Give me your love
Give it to me
Give it to me

Don't you know that I care about you
But I just can't wait?
Give it
Give it to me

Look at me while I tell you 'bout love
Don't you know that you should never doubt love?
With you near I feel you warm inside
When it comes to the real thing there's no compromise

When you're lying next to me
I just get the urge to consummate ecstasy
When I look into your eyes
I can see the fire of desire reflect to me
Give me your love
Give it to me
Give it to me
Aw
Give me your love
Give it to me
Give it to me

Don't you know that I care about you
But I just can't wait?
Don't you know that I care about you
So why should we hesitate?
After all we're in love with each other
So why should we wait?
Give it
Give it to me

God, What Have I Done?

Breakfast in the room was continental
So went to find a small café
Latin lovers can be temperamental
You have to be careful what you say

God, what have I done?

Trying hard to leave the past behind me
Hoping to avoid the same mistake
Haunting memories that still remind me
How lonely is the road that I must take

God, what have I done?
Everything seems strange
God, what have I done?
Everything seems strange

Guess I Must Have Been In Love With Myself

Right from the start
I played my part
In this show
What if today
Was yesterday?
Who would know?
Take your time don't worry
There's no need to hurry
Anything can happen given time

Out of the blue
It came to me
What to do
Funny to say
It was that way
Now it's you
Take your time don't worry
There's no need to hurry
Anything can happen given time

You look at me while I'm looking at you
There's nothing in this world that we two couldn't do
I speak of love in a passionate way
Love is emotion, what more can I say?
The rate of change is a sign of the times
I have no need to read between the lines
I had no time for anyone else
Guess I must have been in love with myself

Everything's changed
Nothing's the same
As before
Thinking of you
Things that you do
Make me so sure

At the moment I feel like walking
Through the pouring rain
Once I get my head together
Nothing will ever be quite the same

You look at me while I'm looking at you
There's nothing in this world that we two couldn't do
I speak of love in a passionate way
Love is emotion, what more can I say?
The rate of change is a sign of the times
I have no need to read between the lines
I had no time for anyone else
Guess I must have been in love with myself

Hold Me Close

You say the world's just going mad
I say that things are not too bad
But it could be better all the same
You know how you want life to be
I know that I may disagree
But neither of us is to blame

Just hold me close don't let me go
I couldn't stand it
You're just what I've been waiting for

You seem to never notice me
I dream that one day you will see
The love meant for both of us to share
You try, you try to be carefree
I smile I know you're just like me
The search for truth's an awesome dare

Just hold me close don't let me go
I couldn't stand it
You're just what I've been waiting for

Just hold me close don't let me go
Not for a minute
You're just what I've been living for

When winter comes and cold winds blow
I'll keep your secret
And if they ask me I don't know
I'll keep your secret
In the middle of the darkest night
Yours will be the light that guides me through
There's no one like you

Just hold me close don't let me go
I couldn't stand it
You're just what I've been waiting for

Just hold me close don't let me go
Not for a minute
You're just what I've been living for

Hollow Inside

Hollow inside I was hollow inside
But I couldn't find out what the reason was
Why I was
Hollow inside I was hollow inside
But I couldn't find out what the reason was
Why I was
Hollow inside I was hollow inside
But I couldn't find out what the reason was
Why I was
Hollow inside I was hollow inside
But I couldn't find out what the reason was
Why I was
Hollow inside
Hollow inside
Hollow inside
Why I was
Hollow inside
Hollow inside
Hollow inside

Hollow inside you were hollow inside
But I couldn't find out what the reason was
Why I was
Hollow inside you were hollow inside
But I couldn't find out what the reason was
Why I was
Hollow inside you were hollow inside
But I couldn't find out what the reason was
Why I was
Hollow inside you were hollow inside
But I couldn't find out what the reason was
Why I was
Hollow inside
Hollow inside
Hollow inside

Why I was
Hollow inside
Hollow inside
Hollow inside

Hollow inside they were hollow inside
But I couldn't find out what the reason was
Why I was
Hollow inside they were hollow inside
But I couldn't find out what the reason was
Why I was
Hollow inside they were hollow inside
But I couldn't find out what the reason was
Why I was
Hollow inside they were hollow inside
But I couldn't find out what the reason was
Why I was
Hollow inside
Hollow inside
Hollow inside
Why I was
Hollow inside
Hollow inside
Hollow inside

Hollow inside we're all hollow inside
But I couldn't find out what the reason was
Why I was
Hollow inside we're all hollow inside
But I couldn't find out what the reason was
Why I was
Hollow inside we're all hollow inside
But I couldn't find out what the reason was
Why I was
Hollow inside we were hollow inside
But I couldn't find out what the reason was

Why I was
Hollow inside
Hollow inside
Hollow inside
Why I was
Hollow inside
Hollow inside
Hollow inside

Homosapien

I'm the shy boy
You're the coy boy
And you know we're
Homosapien too
I'm the cruiser
You're the loser
Me and you sir
Homosapien too
Homo superior
In my interior
But from the skin out
I'm Homosapien too
And you're Homosapien too
And I'm Homosapien like you
And we're Homosapien too

And I think of your eyes in the dark and I see the star
And I look to the light and I might wonder right where you are
All the gods in the sky way up high see the earth spinning round
But the sun and the moon and the stars are so far from the ground

I'm the shy boy
You're the coy boy
And you know we're
Homosapien too
I'm the cruiser
You're the loser
Me and you sir
Homosapien too
Homo superior
In my interior
But from the skin out
I'm Homosapien too
And you're Homosapien too
And I'm Homosapien like you
And we're Homosapien too

And the worlds built of age are a stage where we act out our lives
And the words in the script seem to fit 'cept we have some surprise
I just want this to last or my future is past and all gone
And if this is the case then I'll lose in life's race from now on

Homo superior
In my interior
But from the skin out
I'm Homosapien too
And you're Homosapien too
And I'm Homosapien like you
And we're Homosapien too

And I just hope and pray that the day of our love is at hand
You and I, me and you, we will be one from two, understand?
And the world is so wrong that I hope that we'll be strong enough
For we are on our own and the only thing known is our love
I don't wanna classify you like an animal in the zoo
But it seems good to me to know that you're Homosapien too

I'm the shy boy
You're the coy boy

I don't wanna classify you like an animal in the zoo
But it seems good to me to know that you're Homosapien too
I don't wanna classify you like no animal in the zoo
But it seems good to me to know that you're Homosapien too
I don't wanna classify you like an animal in the zoo
But it seems good to me to know that you're Homosapien too

I Believe

In these times of contention it's not my intention to make things plain
I'm looking through mirrors to catch the reflection that can't be mine
I'm losing control now I'll just have to slow down a thought or two
I can't feel the future and I'm not even certain that there is a past

I believe in the Worker's Revolution
And I believe in the Final Solution
I believe in
I believe in
I believe in the shape of things to come
And I believe in I'm not the only one
Yes I believe in
I believe in

When I poison my system I take thoughts and twist them into shapes
I'm reaching my nadir and I haven't an idea of what to do
I'm painting by numbers but can't find the colours that fill you in
I'm not even knowing if I'm coming or going if to end or begin

I believe in the Immaculate Conception
And I believe in the Resurrection
And I believe in
I believe in
I believe in the elixir of youth
And I believe in the absolute truth
Yes I believe in
I believe in

There is no love in this world anymore
There is no love in this world anymore

I've fallen from favour while trying to savour experience
I'm seeing things clearly but it has quite nearly blown my mind
It's the aim of existence to offer resistance to the flow of time
Everything is and that is why it is will be the line

I believe in perpetual motion
And I believe in perfect devotion
I believe in
I believe in
I believe in the things I've never had
I believe in my Mum and my Dad
And I believe in
I believe in

There is no love in this world anymore
There is no love in this world anymore

I'm skippin' the pages of a book that takes ages for the foreword to end
Triangular cover concealing another aspect from view
My relative motion is just an illusion from stopping too fast
The essence of being, these feelings I'm feeling, I just want them to last

I believe in Original Sin
And I believe what I believe in
Yes I believe in
I believe in
I believe in the web of fate
And I believe in I'm going to be late
So I'll be leavin'
What I believe in

There is no love in this world anymore
There is no love in this world anymore
There is no love in this world anymore
There is no love in this world anymore
There is no love in this world anymore
There is no love in this world anymore
There is no love in this world anymore
There is no love in this world anymore
There is no love in this world anymore
58   There is no love in this world anymore

There is no love in this world anymore
There is no love in this world anymore
There is no love in this world anymore
There is no love in this world anymore
There is no love in this world anymore
There is no love in this world anymore

I Don't Exist

I wonder if you'll notice
Exactly how I feel?
Maybe if we could spend more time together
Then you'd discover what I try hard to conceal

But you don't know what I'm talking about

I kinda get so excited
And I break into a sweat
I wish that I could stage the perfect encounter
That I just hope to God I won't live to regret

But you don't know what I'm talking about
'Cause to you, I just don't exist

But you don't know what I'm talking about
'Cause to you, I just don't exist
But you don't know what I'm talking about
'Cause to you, well, I just don't exist

But you don't know what I'm talking about

I Don't Know What Love Is

I don't know what it is but
It makes me feel I'm crazy
I don't know what it is but
It makes reality hazy
I don't know what it is but
I got the feeling that it might be love

I don't know what it is but
It's a feelin' that moves me
I don't know what it is but
It sends a shiver running through me
I don't know what it is but
I got the feeling that it might be love
It might be love

I don't know what it is but
It makes my heart beat faster
I don't know what it is but
It has become my master
I don't know what it is but
It has taken control an', an', I
I don't know what it is but
It's taken my very heart and soul

I don't know what it is but
It's this feelin' that moves me
I don't know what it is but
It sends these shivers running through me
I don't know what it is but
I got the feeling that it might be love
I don't know what it is but
I got the feeling that it might be love
I don't know what it is but
I got the feeling that it might be love
I don't know what it is but
I got the feeling that it might be love

I Don't Know What To Do With My Life

I don't know what to do with my life
Should I give it up and make a new start?
I don't know what to do with my life
'Cos the one I've got just tears me apart
I can't wake up in the morning
And I can't get to sleep at night
I'm not expecting things to be perfect
But a high success rate would be nice

I don't know what to do with my life
I don't know what to do with my life
I don't know what to do with my life
I don't know what to do with my life

I don't know what's gone wrong with my life
But you know I never do seem to win
Whenever I think I've straightened it out
It becomes a vicious circle again
I can't love when anyone loves me
And I can't find the someone to love
But then I start to count my blessings
And I feel I'm getting more than enough

I don't know what to do with my life
I don't know what to do with my life
I don't know what to do with my life
I don't know what to do with my life

I don't know what to do with my life
I don't know what to do with my life
I don't know what to do with my life
I don't know what to do with my life

I don't know what's gone wrong with my life
But you know I never do seem to win
Whenever I think I've straightened it out
It becomes a vicious circle again
I can't love when anyone loves me
And I can't find the someone to love
But then I start to count my blessings
And I feel I'm getting more than enough of love

I don't know what to do with my life
I don't know what to do with my life
I don't know what to do with my life
It's my life

I Don't Mind

Reality's a dream
A game in which I seem
To never find out just what I am
I don't know if I'm an actor or ham
A shaman or sham
But if you don't mind
I don't mind

I'm lost without a clue
So how can I undo
The tangle of these webs I keep weaving?
I don't know if I should be believing
Deceptive perceiving
But if you don't mind
I don't mind

I used to bet that you didn't care
But gambling never got me anywhere
Each time I used to feel so sure
Something about you made me doubt you more

How can you convince me
When everything I see
Just makes me feel you're putting me down?
And if it's true this pathetic clown'll
Keep hanging around
That's if you don't mind
I don't mind

I used to bet that you didn't care
But gambling never got me anywhere
Each time I used to be so sure
Something about you made me doubt you more

I even think you hate me when you call me on the phone
And sometimes when we go out then I wish I'd stayed at home

And when I'm dreaming or just lying in my bed
I think you've got it in for me
Is it all in my head?
Is it in my head?

How can you convince me
When everything I see
Just makes me feel you're putting me down?
And if it's true this pathetic clown'll
Keep hanging around
That's if you don't mind
I don't mind
I don't mind

I Generate A Feeling

When I close my eyes I have a world inside of me
Peopled by my thoughts of you and how things ought to be
Here I spend my time and do the things I want to do
Helps to pass the day and it keeps me happy too

I, I, I generate a feeling

In my psychic scenery there's a special place I go
Here I am recharged with energy from down below
Nothing is between all we feel is just inside
Generate that feeling and the world will come alive

I, I, I generate a feeling

Listening to the rhythm that I hear within my brain
Everything is different my perceptions aren't the same
When I can't believe the wonder that surrounds me
I just reach deep inside and switch on my euphoria

I, I, I generate a feeling
I, I, I generate a feeling

I Just Wanna Touch

I don't wanna maul you at all, you know
I kinda like you too much
It would be great if we could relate this way, 'cos I
I just wanna touch

I don't wanna play the old roles, you know
Like taking turns to be butch
Don't want our love to be over in minutes and so I
I just wanna touch

Oh, I wonder if you understand
That oh, just having you near
Is better than all of those one night stands?

I hope that you don't get me wrong, you see
I'm not perverted as such
Just wanna love that is more than mere fantasy, so I
I just wanna touch

I, I just wanna
I, I just wanna
I, I just wanna touch
I, I just wanna
I, I just wanna
I, I just wanna touch

Oh, I wonder if you understand
That oh, just having you near
Is better than all of those one night stands?

I don't wanna maul you at all, you know
I kinda like you too much
It would be great if we could relate this way, 'cos I
I just wanna touch

I, I just wanna
I, I just wanna
I, I just wanna touch
I, I just wanna
I, I just wanna
I, I just wanna touch

I Look Alone

I am alone there's nobody there
I have some time to spare
Whenever I feel this way
I look around at everyone else
Have they no time to spare
Whenever I feel this way?

Oh today is beautiful
Tomorrow's beautiful
Everything's beautiful

I look alone I'm left on the shelf
I've got the time to spare
Whenever I feel this way
You look alone there's nobody else
Have you no time to spare
Maybe you feel this way?

Oh today is beautiful
Tomorrow's beautiful
Everything's beautiful

Oh today is beautiful
Tomorrow's beautiful
Everything's beautiful

Don't be alone with nobody there
I have the time to spare
Whenever you feel this way
Why be alone? Come down off the shelf
We have the time to spare
So why should we feel this way?

Oh today is beautiful
Tomorrow's beautiful
Everything's beautiful

You look alone there's nobody else
We have the time to spare
Whenever we feel this way
Let's be alone we need no one else
And we've got lots to share
Whenever we get this way

Oh today is beautiful
Tomorrow's beautiful
Everything's beautiful

Oh today is beautiful
Tomorrow's beautiful
Everything's beautiful

Oh today is beautiful

I Need

I need
I need
I need
I need

I used to only want but now I need
To get by with what I got but now I need
I need
I used to only want but now I need

I need sex
I need love
I need drink
I need drugs
I need food
I need cash
I need you to love me back

I need
I need
I need
I need

I just can't do without 'cos now I need
The things I care about 'cos now I need
I need
I used to only want but now I need

I need sex
I need love
I need drink
I need drugs
I need food
I need cash
I need you to love me back

I need
I need
I need
I need

And now I have to dream because I need
Of a necessary scheme to get me what I need
I need
I used to only want but now I need

I need
I need
I need
I need

The things I used to crave for now I need
Have made me just a slave for what I need
I need
Yes I am just a slave for what I need

I need sex
I need love
I need flu
I need drugs
I need food
I need cash
I need you to love me back
You to love me back
You to love me back

I Surrender

Life's like a lazy river
As you slowly drift downstream
I find myself reminded
Just what you mean to me
The past will never leave me
The future's already here
I imagine there's no escaping
My deep-seated fear

I always thought you were my only friend
When I told you that I loved you did you understand?
Don't wanna count on fishes in the sea
But at the time I saw the sign of how you wanted things to be

I surrender
With no regret
Just remember
Life's not over yet

I feel you when I'm dreaming
So soft against my skin
There's no need to feel so guilty
There's no element of sin
As you reach your own conclusion
I began to lose control
Is the method in my madness
Like the sadness in my soul?

I always thought you were my only friend
When I told you that I loved you did you understand?
Don't wanna count on fishes in the sea
But at the time I saw the sign of how you wanted things to be

I surrender
With no regret
Just remember
Life's not over yet

I always thought you were my only friend
When I told you that I loved you did you understand?
Don't wanna count on fishes in the sea
But at the time I saw the sign of how you wanted things to be
And though you're gone I carry on though all that's left's the memory

I surrender
With no regret
Just remember
Life's not over yet

I've Had Enough

This time I've made up my mind
I've had enough
What a complete waste of time
I've had enough

Each morning I wake to discover
That nothing's changed
The love I wished for don't exist
If it's not one thing it's another
Can't carry on
But I feel powerless to resist

Friends don't know what I go through
I've had enough
Now see what you've made me do
I've had enough

Been trapped in this state of denial
For far too long
The love I've aimed for has been missed
But this time I'm serious, it's final
It would be wrong
Don't wanna be a masochist

And I wish that there could be another way
But I can't believe a single word you say
Anyway

Not gonna take any more
I've had enough
Just what did you take me for?
I've had enough

Each morning I wake and discover
You're still the same
The love I crave for won't exist

It's neither one thing nor another
I won't go on
I hope I'll find strength to resist

Yes, it's the end of the line
I've had enough

If You Ask Me (I Won't Say No)

I can't sleep
My dreams are dreamless
Something's going on between us
I'm too nervous though to make the first move
All I need is your attention
Love's so very hard to mention
Especially when we're just supposed to be friends

You look to me like you've got all the answers
Here's something else you should know
If you ask me I won't say no
If you ask me I won't say no

Small talk always sounds familiar
If I make a pass won't you?
Will you?
I couldn't stand to have to start over again
I react to your reaction
I'm attracted by your attraction
Don't see why we cannot be lovers as friends

I'm not saying that I've got all the answers
But I can tell you this though
If you ask me I won't say no
If you ask me I won't say no

I'm not being backward coming forward
Just sideway's my style
Instead of me just inching closer
Won't you give me a sign?

The cause of my misapprehension
My deep-seated fear of rejection
Help me to express the affection I feel

I'm not being backward coming forward
Just sideway's my style
Instead of me just inching closer
Won't you give me a sign?

And what's the point in me pretending
That I don't mind?
You need only to ask me the question
And I'll be by your side

If you ask me I won't say no
If you ask me I won't say no

In Love With Somebody Else

Everybody's coming to me
For some love, oh yeah
I'm popular since you left me you see
All booked up, oh yeah
But half of what I want I don't need
'Cos you see
I'm in love with somebody else
With a dream whose passion's a dare
And I'm always so unaware

Crazy people coming to me
For their love, oh yeah
Nothing's paid so they think it's free
So they think, oh yeah
I bet they'll leave this ship if it sinks
They don't see
That they're in love with somebody else
With a dream whose passion's a dare
And they're all so, so unaware

I used to think that you were my love
But now I know I was mistaken
But love is what I feel in heart
I may be lonely but I am not forsaken

One day I'll be coming to you
For my love oh, yeah
You're the only one thoughts are of
All the time oh, yeah
But don't take it to heart when you find
That it's true
That you're in love with somebody else
With a dream whose passion's a dare
And you're always so unaware

You're in love
In love
In love with somebody else

Innocent

I thought you were so innocent
Until I got my fingers burnt
You think me strange and quite peculiar
Let the first appearance fool ya
Even though you're not my mum
I've got to get my washing done
Who calls the tune must pay the piper
Fix the plug and catch the spider

Something hesitated in the sky
When I found you
Something emanated from your eyes
My dream came true

I love someone who looks like you
The way you do but isn't you
It's still the same sad sordid story
Suffering sinner slave to glory
Now you say you want someone new
I knew you do you left a clue
The vows of love that you've recanted
Say you're taking me for granted

Something hesitated in the sky
When I found you
Something emanated from your eyes
My dream came true

Innocent
Innocent

Something hesitated in the sky
When I found you
Something emanated from your eyes
My dream came true

Innocent
Innocent

Something hesitated in the sky
When I found you
Something emanated from your eyes
My dream came true

Something hesitated in your eyes
When I found you
Something emanated from the sky
My dream came true

It's Hard Enough Knowing

It's hard enough knowin'
And harder still showin'
What you feel when you're in love
Well it's okay you say it plain
But I don't mind it's all a game

It's hard to believe in
That you've been deceivin'
Me with all of your lies
I don't know what I ought to do
But I know that I still love you

I've given up wishin'
For what has been missin'
When I've looked in your eyes
You know that it's all up to you
There's nothing else that I can do

In my heart I am prayin'
That you will be stayin'
Here with me by my side
I don't want it to end this way
What else more can I say?

It's hard enough knowin'
And harder still showin'
What you feel when you're in love
Well it's okay you say it plain
But I don't mind it's all a game

It's hard to believe in
That you've been deceivin'
Me with all of your lies
I don't know what I ought to do
But I know that I still love you

It's Not You

It's not you
So I close my eyes
It's not you
So I fantasise
It's not you
So I'm on my own now
What am I living for?

It's not you
So I feel the pain
It's not you
So it's not the same
It's not you
So I'm on my own now
What am I living for?

It's not you
It's not you

It's not you
So I count the cost
It's not you
So I feel the loss
It's not you
So I'm on my own now
What am I living for?

It's not you
It's not you
It's not you
It's not you

It's not you
So I'm stripped of pride
It's not you
So I'm dead inside

It's not you
So I'm on my own now
What am I living for?

It's not you
It's not you
It's not you
It's not you

Jerk

Yesterday while feeling down
I called you on the phone
Instead of being warm
You seemed so cold
Was it something that I said
Or something on your mind?
No matter what it was
We had a row

Believe me
I'm sorry
I never meant to argue
I'm a jerk you're right to tell me so
Forgive me
I beg you
You know I only love you
Wish I hadn't told you where to go

It was my fault, you're not to blame
It's me who's in the wrong
That's why I wrote this song just to explain
Accept my apology
It comes straight from my heart
Let's put it all behind us and move on

Believe me
I'm sorry
I never meant to argue
I'm a jerk you're right to tell me so
Forgive me
I beg you
You know I only love you
Wish I hadn't told you where to go

Believe me
I'm sorry
I never meant to argue
I'm a jerk you're right to tell me so
Forgive me
I beg you
You know I only love you
Wish I hadn't told you where to go

Believe me
I'm sorry
I never meant to argue
I'm a jerk you're right to tell me so
I beg you
Forgive me
You know I only love you
Wish I hadn't told you where to go

Just One Of Those Affairs

I always thought you would
I always knew you could
My mind had the idea running through it
I always thought you might
Sometimes but not just quite
But now we're right baby let's do it

Do it on the landing baby
Do it on the stairs
Don't mind the cat
He licks his paws and purrs
I bet this time
I've taken you unawares
But after all you know
It's just only one of those affairs

One of those affairs
One of those oooh yeah
One of those affairs now

I always thought you would
I always knew you could
My mind had the idea running through it
I always thought you might
Sometimes but not just quite
But now we're right baby let's do it

Do it like a lion, baby
Do it in our lairs
Do it like the birds and bees
And Arctic polar bears
Do it when I'm sleepin'
I'm doing it in my prayers
To God in Heaven above
It's just only one of those affairs

One of those affairs
One of those oooh yeah
One of those affairs now

Do it like a lion baby
Do it in our lairs
Do it like the birds and bees
And Arctic polar bears
Do it when I'm sleepin'
I'm doing it in my prayers
To God in Heaven above
It's just only one of those affairs

One of those affairs
One of those oooh yeah
One of those affairs now

One of those affairs
One of those oooh ow
One of those affairs

Keats' Song

I never knew that
Party talk is oh so dull
Oh what fun to chat
No thanks my glass is full
I looked in your eyes
And blushed with surprise

I'd met you before
Hello I beg you pardon
Couldn't hear 'bove the roar
Why not let's go in the garden?
You led the way
Oh my it's my day

We looked at a flower
Night-scented so you said
We talked for an hour
Or more and then you read
From the book of my mind
Some words of poetry of a kind

We said our goodbyes
'Au revoir', they say in French
My taxi rolled by
I slouched on the upholstered bench
Oh Keats was so clever
A thing of beauty is a joy for ever

Keep On

There's no two ways about it
There's nothing left to say
If you only paid attention
Then things wouldn't be this way
Crazy-paved with good intentions
Is the rut that you're stuck in
So that all that's left to fear
Is the enemy within

Suffer from a little depression baby
Gotta tell the world what you feel
Nothing wrong with self-expression baby
Keep on keeping it real

Spare me your hypocrisy
I haven't got the time
For unreasonable reason's
More a punishment than crime
We all can take cold comfort
Now the writing's on the wall
But the pill that's left to swallow
Is the bitterest of all

Suffer from a little depression baby
Gotta tell the world what you feel
Nothing wrong with self-expression baby
Keep on keeping it real
One more Pyrrhic victory
Another dodgy deal

Suffer from a little depression baby
Gotta tell the world what you feel
Nothing wrong with self-expression baby
Keep on keeping it real

Suffer from a little depression baby
Gotta tell the world what you feel
One more Pyrrhic victory
Another dodgy deal
Nothing wrong with self-expression baby
Keep on keeping it real
One more Pyrrhic victory
Another dodgy deal

Suffer from a little depression baby
Gotta tell the world what you feel
Don't jump to confusion
It's all a wind up
Nothing wrong with self-expression baby
Keep on keeping it real
Don't jump to confusion
It's all a wind up

Keep On Believing

Tell me what I need to know
And show me what you got to show
I go with the flow
Keep on believing

It's good enough for rock and roll
If you feel it in your heart and soul
Then you're in control
Keep on believing

Are you smiling, are you frowning
Waving or drowning?
There's too much going on just to ignore
What's the use complaining
That it's forever raining?
After all that's what they make umbrellas for

No matter what they say
You're gonna do it anyway
There's a price to pay
Keep on believing

In the middle of the night
It's dark, but don't lose sight
There's no wrong or right
Keep on believing

And when your only trouble
Is the bursting of the bubble
Remember that there's nothing left to fear
Don't let your consternation
Spoil this celebration
Just ask yourself 'What's the big idea?'

Are you smiling, are you frowning
Waving or drowning?
There's too much going on just to ignore
What's the use complaining
That it's forever raining?
After all that's what they make umbrellas for

Now I don't wanna make it worse
Time's forward no reverse
From the cradle to the hearse
Keep on believing

Don't want for it to end
I need someone to call a friend
On whom I can depend
Keep on believing

I don't want to spoil your day
But I'm gonna say it anyway
There's a price to pay
Keep on believing

Kiss 'N' Tell

You should write a book
I remember the times you wanted ten pence for a look
Which you took

I'm under your spell
Go on then kiss 'n' tell
Take what you can sell
Go on now kiss 'n' tell
Log on to the well
Go for it kiss 'n' tell
Come on now 'kin 'ell you want to
Just kiss 'n' tell

So tired
My home contents insurance has just expired
Unrequired

I'm under your spell
Go on then kiss 'n' tell
Take what you can sell
Go on now kiss 'n' tell
Log on to the well
Go for it kiss 'n' tell
Come on now 'kin 'ell you want to
Just kiss 'n' tell

Power without guilt
Is like love without doubt
Secrets will in time find a way out
As a shout

New York
Why not go for a walk in Central Park
After dark?

I'm under your spell
Go on then kiss 'n' tell
Take what you can sell
Go on now kiss 'n' tell
Log on to the well
Go for it kiss 'n' tell
Come on now 'kin 'ell you want to
Just kiss 'n' tell

Kiss 'n' tell
Kiss 'n' tell
Kiss 'n' tell

Last To Know

Will I be the last to know?
I've got this little question for ya
Will I be the last to know
Or is this just my paranoia?
Will I be the last to know?

I came into your room while you were sleeping
And tip-toed to the bottom of your bed
I held my breath so I could hear you breathing
Love's such a sweet thing

Will I be the last to know?
I've got this little question for ya
Will I be the last to know
Or is this just my paranoia?
Will I be the last to know?

I want to give myself to you completely
I love you more than truth could ever tell
Please promise not to mistreat me or beat me
Just treat me sweetly

Will I be the last to know?
I've got this little question for ya
Will I be the last to know
Or is this just my paranoia?

What will I discover
Will you turn on me and say
You didn't mean to be unkind
You haven't changed your mind
You never loved me anyway?

I want to give myself to you completely
I love you more than truth could ever tell

Please promise not to mistreat me or beat me
Just treat me sweetly

Will I be the last to know?
I've got this little question for ya
Will I be the last to know
Or is this just my paranoia?

What will I discover
Will you turn on me and say
You haven't changed your mind
You've never loved me anyway?

Will I be the last to know?
Will I be the last to know?
Will I be the last to know?

Libertine Angel

They don't make the future
Like they did in the past
Shedding scant light
On the darkness of life
It's like you're making outrageous demands
And all my ancestors
Were Primitive Man
Just look what you've got
Admit you've lost the plot
It's something we can all understand

There's no turning back now
It's out of control
Take away history
You're left with a mystery
Life sentence no chance of parole

No need to be nervous
We'll never get caught
It's my advice
That if you've paid the price
Then don't forget to take what you've bought

See the sword of the people
A libertine angel
The sword of the people
A libertine angel
Be an angel

There's no turning back now
It's out of control
Take away history
You're left with a mystery
Life sentence no chance of parole
And all my ancestors

Were primitive, man
Just look what you've got
Admit you've lost the plot
It's like something we could all understand

See the sword of the people
A libertine angel
The sword of the people
A libertine angel
Be an angel
The sword of the people
A libertine angel
The sword of the people
A libertine angel
Be an angel
Be an angel
Be an angel

Life Without Reason

One by one
Counting the stars in the sky
I thought millions of people will die
Eventually

Life without reason
Just can't be believed in

On and on
Circling round in my head
As soon as you are born you are dead
You know that

Life without reason
Just can't be believed in
You know that for everything
There is a season

I think about it every day
There's no escaping it anyway

Start today
Live every hour as your last
You see the future's as dead as the past
Believe me

Life without reason
Just can't be believed in
You know that for everything
There is a season

Lipstick

When you kiss me
Does the lipstick on your lip stick on my face?
Will you miss me?
In your dreams does your lover have my face?

Ah when you kiss me
Does the lipstick on your lip stick on my face?
Ah will you miss me?
In your dreams does your lover have my face?

It's the morning
And the mourning it is dawning on me too
I'd no warning
Just a condolence card to tell me that we're through

Ah it's the morning
And the mourning it is dawning on me too
I had no warning
Just a condolence card to tell me that we're through

Will you kiss me?
Does the lipstick on your lip stick on my face?
When you miss me
In your dreams does my lover have your face?

Ah when you kiss me
Does the lipstick on your lip stick on my face?
Ah will you miss me?
In your dreams does your lover have my face?

Look At You Now

Don't go acting all innocent
It suits you way too much
I know the messages we've sent
Have helped us get in touch

There was a time you showed me the pictures
Butter wouldn't melt in your mouth
But now let's skip to the future
Look at you now

Don't want you making no big mistake
Especially when it's dark
Not to mention the risk you take
While drinking in the park

There was a time you showed me the pictures
Butter wouldn't melt in your mouth
But now let's skip to the future
Look at you now

There was a time you showed me the pictures
Butter wouldn't melt in your mouth
But now let's skip to the future
Look at you now

The triumph of hope over experience
My faith has been restored
An uncommon sense of common sense
Sure is its own reward

There was a time you showed me the pictures
Butter wouldn't melt in your mouth
But now let's skip to the future
Look at you now

There was a time you showed me the pictures
Butter wouldn't melt in your mouth
But now let's skip to the future
Look at you now

Don't go acting all innocent
Look at you now

Love In Vain

For quite a long time
I was making hard what's easy
I was running round in circles
When I bumped into you
Don't tell me that my love's in vain

I've had a second chance
And there's still a million others
Have I been fooling myself
To think that I could fool you?
Don't tell me that my love's in vain

Oh, worries all around
It's getting dark there's no denying
But just above the clouds
The sky is blue, the sun's shining

I've had too much of dreamin'
I'm gonna keep my eyes wide open
Better not believin'
Than believe what's not true
Don't tell me that my love's in vain

If you make up your mind
Would I change so I would notice?
Oh, won't you tell me
What I ought to do?
Don't tell me that my love's in vain

Oh, worries all around
It's getting dark there's no denying
But just above the clouds
The sky is blue, the sun's shining
Don't tell me that my love's in vain

You had a second chance
And there's still a million others
You may be fooling yourself
But you don't fool me too
Don't tell me that my love's in vain

Don't tell me that my love's in vain
Don't tell me that my love's in vain
Don't tell me that my love's in vain
Don't tell me that my love's in vain
Don't tell me that my love's in vain

Love You More

I'm in love again
Been like this before
I'm in love again
This time's true I'm sure

Don't wanna end up like no nine-day wonder
I've been hurt so many times before
So my darlin' I will never leave you
It's in my blood to always love you more
Love you more

It's my heart again
That drives me so wild
I just can't explain
Although I'm not a child

So why would I cry if you ever left me?
Maybe 'cos you're all I'm livin' for
With every heartbeat I want you madly
It's in my blood to always love you more
Love you more

Oh my love again
What I say is true
Though it may sound plain
I love you

And it means more to me than life can offer
And if this isn't true love then I am sure
That after this love there'll be no other
Until the razor cuts

Many A Time

I seem to pack my mind
With useless information
Until it drags me down
You seem to fill the time
With useless occupations
Until it drags you down
I've had my share
Of broken promise dreaming
Until it dragged me down
Why should I wait
Another lonely lifetime
Until it drags me down?

I'm more and more amazed by the world that I see
I'm quite convinced though that this is all happening to me

Many a time I've tried concealing
Looking the other way
Many a time I've tried believing
Living from day to day
Many a time I've lied deceiving
Many a time

Why must we wait until a revolution
Before we drag it down?
It's not too late to resolve the old solution
And then we'll drag it down

I'm more and more amazed by the world that I see
I'm quite convinced though that this is all happening to me

Many a time I've tried concealing
Looking the other way
Many a time I've tried believing
Living from day to day
Many a time I've lied deceiving
Many a time

I'm more and more amazed by the world that I see
I'm quite concerned though that this is all happening to me

Many a time I've tried

Maxine

Am I awake or trapped inside
Somebody else's dream?
Oh Maxine
Is this all real or dope-induced
Are things as they all seem?
Oh Maxine

I've never been in love before
At least not in this kind
I've seldom felt such happiness
But if I am really in love then
Why is it me because
I didn't think that I was your kind?
Not good enough for your love

You see the shape I know I'm in
With only you to blame
Oh Maxine
The life I led is long since dead
I do myself resign
To you Maxine

I've never been in love before
At least not in this kind
I've seldom felt such happiness
But if I am really in love then
Why is it me because
I didn't think that I was your kind?
Not good enough for your love
But c'est la vie so divine
Que sera, sera
What will be will be

I've never been in love before
At least not in this kind
I've seldom felt such happiness
But if I am really in love then
Why is it me because
I didn't think that I was your kind?
Not good enough for your love
But c'est la vie so divine
Que sera, sera
What will be will be

Oh Maxine
I love you
Maxine I love you
Oh Maxine
Oh Maxine

(Millions Of People) No One Like You

Stupid things keep on happening
Every single day
When I fall in love
It slips away
Finding out was so hard to take
There's no reason why
When I phoned you up
You said goodbye

You say love's dead and gone
I just carry on
What else can I do?
Maybe I don't know right from wrong
Who knows who cares now?
What else can I do?

Yesterday I kept wishing that
You had changed your mind
Now I guess that it's
All up to you
Am I just today another one
That you've left behind
Or did you love me
With a love so true?

I thought you and I were friends
Still you made me cry
What else can I do?
'N' maybe love will find a way
Give me one more try
It's all up to you

How can you tell me that I must be dreaming?
You're waiting around I've got nothing to do
So tired of waiting I've only one lifetime
There's millions of people but no one like you

I thought you and I were friends
Still you made me cry
What else can I do?
'N' maybe love will find a way
Give me one more try
It's all up to you

How can you tell me that I must be dreaming?
You're waiting around I've got nothing to do
So tired of waiting I've only one lifetime
There's millions of people but no one like you

Money

What is inside me
Is caged here beside me
Life is a zoo
I'm labelled him
And it's labelled you
Life is a zoo
Life's a zoo

You are a stranger
But I'm even stranger
What can I do?
Life's getting stranger
Strangers are stranger
What can we do?
Life's a zoo

I am a stranger
And you're even stranger
What can you do?
Life's getting stranger
A stranger's a stranger
What can we do?
Life's a zoo

Morning After

Sun streams through the window
It's another day
I lie in bed nursing my hangover
Couldn't stomach breakfast
I feel like throwing up

Wake up and face the morning after
Wake up and face the morning after

The switch to double brandies
Was a big mistake
Now my mouth tastes like the bottom of a birdcage
It's nature's way of telling me
That I had better stop

Wake up and face the morning after
Wake up and face the morning after

Moving Away From The Pulsebeat

You said the things you did in the past
Were all because you're living too fast
But now I'm here you're taking it slow
You know what you know you know you know now
I only want to be with you
You do, you do, you do, you do too
You do, you do, you do, you do too
But I'm so happy just to be with you
I knew what you knew what you knew you knew too
Aw

You said that time you didn't love me
Although I'd been the cutest you'd seen
But would the past have changed even though
You know what you know you know you know now
I only want you by my side
Some kinds of pride I just can't hide
Some kinds of pride just can't be denied
But I know that oh no, no, no

My Dreams

I see your face everywhere I go
I feel you behind me
I turn but you're not there
I call your name
And people stop and stare
It's been some time since we last met
How can I forget you?
It came as news to me
Love has no guarantee

Aw, I guess my dreams weren't meant to be
Oh, I guess my dreams weren't meant to be
Parting's not such sweet a sorrow
But who knows how today will be

December will never seem the same
I'll always remember
Being close to you
The colour of your eyes
My favourite shade of blue
Been thinking of the fun we shared
Of course there were bad times
But perhaps what's good for me
Was all the same to you

Aw, I guess my dreams weren't meant to be
Oh, I guess my dreams weren't meant to be
Parting's not such sweet a sorrow
But who knows how today will be?

Calm down
Take it easy
It's not the end of the world
But the chance to start something new

They say time waits for no man
But as long as I live
I'll wait for ever and ever for you

It's been some time since we last met
It was on my birthday
I'll never forget you
Though I suppose eventually I will

Aw, I guess my dreams weren't meant to be
Aw, I guess my dreams weren't meant to be
Parting's not such sweet a sorrow
But who knows how today will be

There are no goodbyes

Calm down
Take it easy
It's not the end of the world
But the chance to start something new
They say time waits for no man
But as long as I live
I'll wait for ever and ever for you
Aw, take it easy
It's not the end of the world
But the chance to start something brand new
They say time waits for no man
But as long as I live
I'll wait for ever and forever for you

Oh, I guess my dreams weren't meant to be
Aw, I guess my dreams weren't meant to be
Aw, I guess my dreams weren't meant to be
Aw, I guess my dreams weren't meant to be

Need A Minit

I need a minute to make my mind up
And you know that time is a sacrifice
In a minute I'll maybe wind up
All the dreams and desires that can't be thought of twice

Everyday I look, every time I see
Don't need a minute to make my mind up
But it's all different now that this is all happening to me
Just need a minute to make my mind up

I need a minute to make my mind up

Everyday I look and every time I see
Don't need a minute to make my mind up
But it's all different now that this is all happening to me
Just need a minute to make my mind up

I need a minute to make my mind up
Wouldn't want to rush into a thing like this
'Cos you know it's the kind of feeling
That you long for so much you cannot resist

Everyday I look, every time I see
Don't need a minute to make my mind up
But it's all different now that this is all happening to me
Just need a minute to make my mind up

I need a minute to make my mind up
Just need a minute to make my mind up
Just need a minute to make my mind up
I need a minute to make my mind up

Just need a minute
Just need a minute
Just need a minute
Just need a minute

Never Again

When I saw you, you were not so happy
So I hung around a while
You said to me 'give me three good reasons
Why I should even raise a smile'
Somebody told me they thought I was a sailor
They thought having fun was the answer
But you see next time could be for ever

The things I say may very well sound different
Depending on your point of view
Some kinds of lovers give you creature comforts
Do anything you want them to
Somebody told me they thought I was much older
They thought having fun was the answer
But you see next time should be for ever

Never again I hear somebody saying
Will you break this heart of mine
But I can't wait not even for a moment
I'm drifting off the edge of time
You showed me things that should remain a mystery
Just like they were intended to
If I try hard and do some rearranging
I could find a place for you

You say you know but you might be mistaken
Taken for a ride again
Alone at last but this is not the first time
I hope it won't turn out the same
Somebody told me they never ever worry
They thought having fun was the answer
But you see next time will last for ever

Never again I hear somebody saying
Will you break this heart of mine
But I can't wait not even for a moment
I'm slipping off the edge of time
You showed me things that should remain a mystery
Just like they were intended to
If I try hard and do some rearranging
I could find a place for you

You told me once but say it again
It's nice to hear you say such sweet things
Hold me close, closer than the last time
It's nice to feel you do such sweet things

Never again I hear somebody saying
Will you break this heart of mine
But I can't wait not even for a moment
I'm dripping off the edges of time
You showed me things that should remain a mystery
Just like they were intended to
If I try hard and do some rearranging
I could find a place for you

Never Believe It

In spite of what I say to you
You never believe it
Especially what I try to do
You never believe it
You never believe it
How can I entreat this to you?

You say that you're not coming back
I couldn't believe it
You near gave me a heart attack
You wouldn't believe it
You wouldn't believe it
How can I believe it's not true?

Of all the things to do
I have to end up took with you
Though I see your face
You're like a monster from another place

You say that you're not coming back
I couldn't believe it
You near gave me a heart attack
You wouldn't believe it
Couldn't believe it
How can I entreat this to you?

In spite of what I say to you
You wouldn't believe it
Especially what I try to do
You never believe it
You never believe it
How can I believe it's not true?

Of all the things to do
I have to end up stuck with you
Though I see your face
You're like a monster from another place

I know I must seem a sucker for your lies
You wouldn't believe it
You wouldn't believe it
But I just love the faraway look in your eyes

Of all the things to do
I have to end up stuck with you
Though I see your face
You're like a monster from another place

Never Gonna Give It Up

Hey there you with your head in the sand
I'm tryna tell you something you'll understand
I wanna spend my time in a passionate way
These feelings keep on growing inside me day by day

The things you do make me so hot
I'd give you everything I've got to give
Let's cut in two the Gordian Knot
Release a power much greater than this foolish pride

Oh no, I'm never gonna give it up
Oh no, I'm never gonna give it up

Hey there you with your head in a cloud
Don't let nobody tell you're not allowed
You'd have no hesitation if only you knew
The sweetness of sensations in store for you

The things you do make me so hot
I'd give you everything I've got to give
Let's cut in two the Gordian Knot
Release a power much greater than this foolish pride

Oh no, I'm never gonna give it up
Oh no, I'm never gonna give it up

The things you do make me so hot
I'd give you everything I've got to give
Let's cut in two the Gordian Knot
Unleash a power much greater than this foolish pride

Oh no, I'm never gonna give it up
Oh no, I'm never gonna give it up
Oh no, I'm never gonna give it up
I'm never ever gonna give it up

No Moon

You're not of this world
You shine above me
I reflect below
You're so familiar
Yet ever changing
You go where I go

But sometimes when I really need you
I look for you and find you've gone

Will I escape from
This empty feeling?
So lonely inside
Could I get thunder
To sing of silence
And surge with the tide?

'Cos sometimes when I really need you
I look for you and find you've gone

I know you'll come back
You won't forsake me
So I'll just carry on

'Cos sometimes when I really need you
I look for you and find you've gone

I know you'll come back
You won't forsake me
So I'll just carry on

No Reply

When I phone you
Night or day
I get no reply
No reply
I'm still writing those letters
And I'm sending them away
To get no reply
No reply

No reply
Oh, can't you see?
No reply
It's ruining me
Even if I
Ask the reason why
I get no reply
No reply
No reply
No reply

Oh no
No, no, no, no, no, no
No reply
No reply
Oh no
No, no, no, no, no, no
No reply
No reply

I'm bruising my knuckles
Knocking at your door
But I get no reply
No reply
I've stood it for so long
But can't stand it no more

To get no reply
No reply

No reply
Oh, can't you see?
No reply
It's ruining me
Even if I
Ask the reason why
I get no reply
No reply
No reply
No reply

Oh no
No, no, no, no, no, no
No reply
No reply
Oh no
No, no, no, no, no, no
No reply
No reply

I'm bruising my knuckles
Knocking at your door
But I get no reply
No reply
I've stood it for so long
But can't stand it no more
To get no reply
No reply

No reply
Oh, can't you see?
No reply
It's ruining me

Even if I
Ask the reason why
I get no reply
No reply
No reply
No reply

Oh no
No, no, no, no, no, no
No reply
No reply
Oh no
No, no, no, no, no, no
No reply
Reply
Reply
Reply

Noise Annoys

Pretty girls
Pretty boys
Have you ever heard your mommy say
'Noise annoys'?

Pretty girls
Pretty boys
Have you ever heard your mommy shout
'Noise annoys!'?

Go

Pretty girls
Pretty boys
Have you ever heard your mommy scream
'Noise annoys!'?

Pretty girls
Pretty boys
Have you ever heard your mommy scream
'Noise annoys!'?

Pretty girls
Pretty boys
Have you ever heard your mommy say
'Noise annoys'?

Nostalgia

I bet that you love me like I love you
But I should know that gambling just don't pay
So I look up to the sky
And I wonder what it'll be like in days gone by
As I sit and bathe in the wave of nostalgia for an age yet to come

I always used to dream of the past
But like they say yesterday never comes
Sometimes there's a song in my brain
And I feel that my heart knows the refrain
I guess it's just the music that brings on nostalgia for an age
    yet to come

Ah, nostalgia for an age yet to come
Nostalgia for an age yet to come

About the future I only can reminisce
For what I've had is what I'll never get
And although this may sound strange
My future and my past are presently disarranged
And I'm surfing on a wave of nostalgia for an age yet to come

I look I only see what I don't know
All that was strong invincible is slain
Takes more than sunshine to make everything fine
And I feel like I'm trapped in the middle of time
And this constant feeling of nostalgia for an age yet to come

Ah, nostalgia for an age yet to come

About the future I only can reminisce
For what I've had is what I'll never get
And although this may sound strange
My future and my past are presently disarranged
And I'm surfing on a wave of nostalgia for an age yet to come

I look I only see what I don't know
All that was strong invincible is slain
Takes more than sunshine to make everything fine
And I feel like I'm caught in the middle of time
And this constant feeling of nostalgia for an age yet to come

Ah, nostalgia for an age yet to come

Nostalgia for an age yet to come
Nostalgia for an age yet to come

Nothing Left

I'm on my own now
You've gone and left me
I bet you don't know
How you've upset me

'Cos I've nothing left at all
At all, at all, at all, at all, at all, at all, at all
I've nothing left at all

Did you love me?
I'd like to think so
But I was blameless
So why did you go?

'Cos I've nothing left at all
At all, at all, at all, at all, at all, at all, at all
I've nothing left at all

I've lost a lover
And I am certain
I'll get another
So why'm I hurtin'?

'Cos I've nothing left at all
At all, at all, at all, at all, at all, at all, at all
I've nothing left at all

'Cos I've nothing left at all
At all, at all, at all, at all, at all, at all, at all
I've nothing left at all

Oh Shit

Oh shit
I thought you and I were friends
Oh shit
I guess this is where our love ends
Oh shit
I thought things were going well
But it hasn't turned out so swell
Has it?
Oh shit

Oh shit
Pride comes before a fall
Oh shit
And once you lose one you've lost them all
Oh shit
I guess this time's the time
And it seems you're no longer mine
Don't it?
Oh shit
Oh shit

Oh shit
I wish I'd known before now
Oh shit
That you were such a cow
Oh shit
I wouldn't've wasted my time
Oh shit
Chasing something which wasn't mine
Face it
You're shit
You're shit

Oh shit
I wish I'd known before now
Oh shit
That you were such a fuckin' cow
Oh shit
I wouldn't've wasted my time
Oh shit
Chasing something which could never be mine
Admit
You're shit
You're shit
You're shit
Admit
Admit
You're shit
You're shit
You're shit
You're shit
You're shit

On Your Own

Tomorrow's just another day
If you can make it through the night
'Cos you're on your own
It's getting darker every minute
Just keep looking for the light
'Cos you're on your own
Sometimes I think it's kinda funny
I just hope it turns out right
'Cos you're on your own

I find it hard to recognise
All these feelings that you try to disguise

I want to tell you not to worry
There's so much that we can do
But you're on your own
There's no use in us pretending
All our alibis have fallen through
You're on your own

I find it hard to recognise
All those feelings that you tried to disguise

Life's a disaster with a heart of stone
You need some affection but you're all alone

You're on your own
You're in control
You come from nowhere
You can't go back there

You're on your own
You're on your own

Do you wake up in the middle of a dream and scream out loud?

Life's a disaster with a heart of stone
You need some affection but you're all alone

You're on your own
You're in control
You come from nowhere
You can't go back there

You're on your own
You're in control
You're on your own
Complete control

Operator's Manual

Operator's manual
Tells me what to do
When emotions blow a fuse
Indicating blue

Operator's manual
Tells me what to find
And how to make adjustments when
You tamper with my mind

Oh, operator's manual
I'd just fall apart without you
If only I had a mechanic
Then somehow I know I'd pull through

Operator's manual
On page sixty-three
Tells me what to do when you
Do these things to me

Oh, operator's manual
I'd just fall apart without you
If only I had a mechanic
Then somehow I know I'd pull through

Operator's manual
Tells me what to do
When emotions blow a fuse
And I'm feeling blue

Operator's manual
On page sixty-three
Tells me what to do when you
Do these things to me

Oh, operator's manual
I'd just fall apart without you
If only I had a mechanic
Then somehow I know I'd pull through

Orion

You and I
Underneath Orion
You and I
Against the bathroom wall
Reminiscing what I'm missing
I can't forget you

You and I

You and I
Entwined forever
You and I
In each other's arms

You and I
Remember?

You and I
We left the lights on
You and I
On an unmade bed
You and I
Just because we want to
Oh, how I miss you

You and I
Remember?

Out Of The Blue

Something's wrong
I don't know what's going on
Just when I thought things were fine
Best left unsaid
The voices in my head
They contradict me all the time

I must confess
My life is in a mess
The best laid plans of mice and men
And when they start
To really fall apart
Can't stick them back again

Out of the blue
Fate knocks at the door
I thought that you knew
But we've both been wrong before
Out of the blue
Wish I could be sure
I hope that it's true
'Cos you keep me wanting more and more and more

Don't get to choose
If we win or lose
Is it all a game of chance?
I can't forget
Those feelings of regret
Instead of sweet romance

I wrote a song
About how things go wrong
You'd think I would have learned by now
Time and again
It's driving me insane

Out of the blue
Fate knocks at the door
I thought that you knew
But we've both been wrong before
Out of the blue
Wish I could be sure
I hope that it's true
'Cos you keep me wanting more and more and more

Something's wrong
I don't know what's going on
Just when I thought things were fine
Best left unsaid
Those voices in my head
That contradict me all the time

I must confess
My life is in a mess
The best laid plans of mice and men
And when they start
They really fall apart

Out of the blue
Fate knocks at the door
I thought that you knew
But we've both been wrong before
Out of the blue
I wish I could be sure
I hope that it's true
'Cos you leave me wanting more and more and more
And more and more and more
And more and more and more
And more and more and more
And more and more

Palm Of Your Hand

It's not so strange you know to feel like this
I thought of you I knew that you'd understand
I think it's time you know we did more than kiss
Ever fallen in love with the palm of your hand?
I've made up my mind as a bull sees red
To get my tail wagged must I sit up and beg?

And if you want to brush up on technique
You can read all about it in the book that I found
When the spirit is willing the flesh won't be weak
There's little more to it than just jerking around
I'm hungry for the most perfect of needs
My craving feeds at the palm of your hand

My temperature shoots up to one hundred degrees
It's manual automatic makes me weak at the knees
My craving feeds at the palm of your hand
Executive attention yes the kind that relieves
You've got the instruments of pleasure at the end of your sleeves
My craving feeds at the palm of your hand
Palm of your hand
The palm of your hand
At the palm of your hand

My temperature shoots up to one hundred degrees
It's manual automatic makes me weak at the knees
My craving feeds at the palm of your hand
Executive attention yes the kind that relieves
You've got the instruments of pleasure at the end of your sleeves
My craving feeds at the palm of your hand
Palm of your hand
The palm of your hand
At the palm of your hand

It's not so strange you know to feel like this
I thought of you I knew that you'd understand
I think it's time you know we did more than kiss
Ever fallen in love with the palm of your hand?
It's practically safe not much risk of disease
My craving feeds at the palm of your hand

My temperature shoots up to one hundred degrees
It's manual automatic makes me weak at the knees
My craving feeds at the palm of your hand
Executive attention yes the kind that relieves
You've got the instruments of pleasure at the end of your sleeves
My craving feeds at the palm of your hand
Palm of your hand
The palm of your hand
At the palm of your hand

Paradise

Where in the world are we?
Everything's fake nothing's real
I guess it just depends on how you feel
Why are you wasting my time
With questions when everything's fine?
Why are things so nice?
Is this the place that they call Paradise?
Oh, it's Paradise

Look around you day by day
See the people on their way
On Friday nights collecting their pay
So don't tell me what's wrong and what's right
'Cos a knife fight on Saturday night
Is the only kind of justice not nice
But it's the only kind that's given here in Paradise
Oh, it's Paradise

Pariah

No one seems to matter anymore
Can't get back to normal like before
Everywhere I look and see the same
Every time I turn around you're back again

Can't you see I'm burning inside?
Can't you see I'm yearning inside?
I'm sick of all this stubborn pride
Pariah, pariah
Pariah, pariah

It seems to me you think that love's a crime
You've taken what is yours and now you're after mine
I'm running round in circles
Nowhere else to go
Hermes Trismegistus
As above so below

Can't you see I'm burning inside?
Can't you see I'm yearning inside?
These feelings cannot be denied
Pariah, pariah
Pariah, pariah
Pariah, pariah
Pariah, pariah

It seems to me you think that love's a crime
You've taken what is yours and now you're after mine
I'm running round in circles
Nowhere else to go
Hermes Trismegistus
As above so below

Can't you see I'm burning inside?
Can't you see I'm yearning inside?
These feelings cannot be denied
Pariah, pariah

Can't you see I'm burning inside?
Can't you see I'm yearning inside?
I'm sick of all this stubborn pride
Pariah, pariah
Pariah, pariah
Pariah, pariah
Pariah, pariah

Phone

At dinner while watching your favourite soap
You'll always return the call
You talk a long time in that certain way
But you don't really say that much at all
You are so close and yet so far away from me
Yes, I get sad
I get sad and lonely
You're all that matters to me

Just put the phone down
Just put the phone down

I know the reason that you can't talk
What's unsaid I guess can keep
What don't you call me on the mobile phone?
After all you know talk is cheap
You are so close and yet so far away from me
Yes, I get sad
I get sad and lonely
You're all that matters to me

Just put the phone down
Just put the phone down
Just put the phone down
Just put the phone down

You are so close and yet so far away from me
Yes, I get sad
I get sad and lonely
You're all that matters to me

Just put the phone down
Just put the phone down
Just put the phone down
Just put the phone down
Just put the phone down

Just put the phone down
Just put the phone down
Just put the phone down

Point Of No Return

If I could discover
One thing or another
I doubt if I'd tremble inside
It ain't paranoia
When they're coming for you
And though you may run you won't hide

The way it should be
Is so wild and so free
That I just don't know which way to turn

Move the world with the power of feeling
And you know we both got a lot to learn
Keep in touch when your senses are reeling
Reach the point of no return

That such sweet sensations
Have their complications
I guess we could read that as read
It will make a difference
Resist your indifference
Or else you'll be better off dead

The way it should be
Is so wild and so free
That I just don't know which way to turn

Move the world with the power of feeling
And you know we both got a lot to learn
Keep in touch when your senses are reeling
Reach the point of no return

Move the world with the power of feeling
And you know we both got a lot to learn
Keep in touch when your senses are reeling
Reach the point of no return

That such sweet sensations
Have their complications
I guess we can read that as read
It will make a difference
Resist your indifference
Or else you'll be better off dead

The way it should be
Is so wild and so free
That I just don't know which way to turn

Move the world with the power of feeling
And you know we both got a lot to learn
Keep in touch when your senses are reeling
Reach the point of no return

Move the world with the power of feeling
And you know we both got a lot to learn
Keep in touch when your senses are reeling
Reach the point of no return

Promises

Ah, loving you is easy you are on my side
We play the game strictly to our rules
We led the field a love affair
Which made all other lovers fools

Oh
How can you ever let me down?
How can you ever let me down?
How can you ever let me down?
These promises are made for us

We promised that we'd always have time for each other
Whenever I needed you'd be there
We promised to be true there'd be no other
We promised that for ever we would care

Oh
How can you ever let me down?
How can you ever let me down?
How can you ever let me down?
These promises are made for us

We had to change
But you stayed the same
You wouldn't change
Oh, what a shame

'Cos loving you's not easy you're not on my side
We play a game with two sets of rules
We lead the field in a love affair
Ah, strictly meant for fools

Oh
Why did you ever let me down?
Why did you ever let me down?
Why did you ever let me down?
Those promises were made for us

You never have any time for me
Whenever I need you, you're not there
You've never been true and it's plain to see
The fact is you never really cared

Oh
Why did you ever let me down?
Why did you ever let me down?
Why did you ever let me down?
Those promises we made for us

Pusher Man

I met a good man
He had some good stuff
He showed me a bag
And he pulled out the snuff
I had just one try
And that was enough
Water poured from my eye
God stuff this rough snuff

I was wiping my eye
On the edge of my sleeve
When who did I spy?
Goddamn, the police!
I said, 'Hey look man the fuzz!'
He turned ghostly white
He gave me the bag
And ran outasight!

I leapt on my hog
And I burned up the street
All the traffic had to stop
'Cos I couldn't be beat
All the people were scared
As they leapt from my wheels
But I didn't care
I couldn't hear their squeals

I went to my pad
And I crashed on my bed
I kept taking that snuff
Until it blew my head
It was really gunpowder
I, a flash in the pan
I, a charcoaled cinder
God damn the pusher man

God damn the pusher man
God damn the pusher man
God damn the pusher man
God damn the pusher man
God damn the pusher man
God damn the pusher man
God damn the pusher man
God damn the pusher man

Qu'Est-Ce Que C'Est Que Ça?

Have you seen them in the skies?
I've been searching
For the things I cannot find
Wishes for me
Wishes for you
Would it makes us happy if our wishes all came true?
Will I ever find the answer

To the questions
That I ask myself sometimes?
Is there a reason
Or is that just in my mind?
Why am I here?
Why are you there?
Are we all that different that there's nothing we can share?
Will I ever find the answer?
Is there even an answer?

Qu'est-ce que c'est que ça?
I wonder who knows?
Qu'est-ce que c'est que ça?
La même chose

Is there anybody out there?

I've been thinking
Do we really have a soul?
Is there a Heaven?
Do you believe all that you're told?
Salvation for you
Damnation for me
Is this all that there is or are there things that we can't see?
Maybe meditation
Could improve my concentration
I need an indication
To establish a relation

Qu'est-ce que c'est que ça?
I wonder who knows?
Qu'est-ce que c'est que ça?
La même chose

And I wonder
I wonder if you wonder too

Qu'est-ce que c'est que ça?
I wonder who knows?
Qu'est-ce que c'est que ça?
La même chose

Qu'est-ce que c'est que ça?
I wonder who knows?
Qu'est-ce que c'est que ça?
La même chose

Raison D'Être

You're an awful lot of fun
Forever on the run
You're my number one
But if you're not late
Then I guess you never come

You're always on my side boy
When it comes to playing games of who are we
We never find out why though
That our own raison d'être we can't see

You're an awful lot of fun
Forever on the run
You're my number one
But if you're not late
Then I guess you never come

I said blue eyes would suit you
Yes, they do
Oh, I knew I would be right
But watch your friends don't get you
'Cos if they do
I won't be seeing you tonight

Real World

I'm in love with the real world
It's mutual or so it seems
'Cos only in the real world
Do things happen like they do in my dreams
Some of the rules may be different
But maybe they'll stay the same
In the real world
In the real world
In the real world
We both win when we play the same game

I'm in love with somebody
I wish somebody loved me too
You may wonder how this concerns you
Well, perhaps the somebody is you
I don't even know what your name is
But I just hope that you'll stay
In the real world
In the real world
In the real world
Things happen this way

I'm in love with somebody
I wish somebody loved me too
You may wonder how this concerns you
Well, perhaps the somebody is you
I don't even know what your name is
But I just hope that you'll stay
In the real world
In the real world
In the real world
We both win when we play the same game

In the real world
In a real world
In a real world
By the way, what's your name?

Reconciliation

Been contemplating lately what you mean to me
You are the one I care about
The only one I love
And though we may be separated by the sea
It's still just you I'm dreaming of
You must believe me

I'm gonna tell you something you already know
'Para sempre' means forever
And I intend to keep that promise, you know?

I have this dream of yearning, burning in my heart
Of how good things still would be if
We made a brand new start
Seven empty days fill weeks
Tough months become long years
But I still cherish memories of romantic beers

And so I'll tell you something you already know
'Para sempre' means forever
I still intend to keep that promise, you know?

What I want is reconciliation
This separation's more than I can bear
Don't wanna be alone,
My love is guaranteed
I want to know that you still care

And so I'll tell you something you already know
'Para sempre' means forever
I still intend to keep my promise, you know?

What I want is reconciliation
This separation's more than I can bear
Don't wanna be alone,
My love is guaranteed
I want to know that you still care

Don't wanna be alone,
My love is guaranteed
I want to know that you still care

No need to be alone
Your love is all I need
Just say the word and I'll be there

Rendezvous

I'd overslept so I caught the bus
It's the only thing I could do
I went upstairs took a vacant seat
And found I'd sat next to you

It's been a long time since we last met
I thought you'd moved out of town
Still have the power to stir me up
Just when I hoped I'd settled down

I'm on a cloud, I must be in a dream
This can't be real, this can't be happening

Before I knew it we had reached your stop
I blurted out something obscene
You promised that you would call me soon
Leave a message on my machine

I'm on a cloud, I must be in a dream
This can't be real, this can't be happening
What are the odds against this rendezvous?
It's worth the gamble when the prize is you

I'm on a cloud, I must be in a dream
This can't be real, this can't be happening
What are the odds against this rendezvous?
It's worth the gamble when the prize is you

Runaround

You send my blood pressure rising
You're driving me crazy
You give me the runaround
Please and I'm not criticising
You're driving me crazy
You give me the runaround

Nobody thrills me like you
I want you all the time
Though I'm patient and I've waited
You give me the runaround
I'm in love trust that it's true
Just give me a sign
God knows I'm dedicated
You give me the runaround

Sex is a bone of contention
You're driving me crazy
You give me the runaround
Love scarcely warrants a mention
You're driving me crazy
You give me the runaround

Confession's good for the soul
And we've both seen better days
I'm gettin' so frustrated
You give me the runaround
Situation's out of control
Gotta be another way
I've desire that must be sated
You give me the runaround

Think of how things ought to be
Reality not fantasy
So certain 'bout the way that I feel
You say you need a guarantee

Just tell me what you want me to see
Oh, how I wish that you would be mine

Sex is a bone of contention
You're driving me crazy
You give me the runaround
Love scarcely warrants a mention
You're driving me crazy
You give me the runaround

Confession's good for the soul
And we've both seen better days
I'm gettin' so frustrated
You give me the runaround
Situation's out of control
Gotta be another way
I've desire that must be sated
You give me the runaround

Think of how things ought to be
Reality not fantasy
So certain 'bout the way that I feel
You say you need a guarantee
Just tell me what you want me to see
Oh, how I wish that you would be mine

Serious Crime

Now you're coming up to meet me
And my heart is beating fast
I once heard that suspicion is a sin
And those little beads of perspiration
Rolling down my back
Just go to show the kind of state I'm in

Now I'm standing in an alley
Finding work for idle hands
On the Day of Judgement no one will be spared
And everything I tell you's
A self-portrait of the blind
'Cos life's a joke and death's the final word
Then everything is clearly absurd

So if you seek, you'll find
Feel like I've been in love since the end of time
So you better get a move on fast
Or we'll all be left behind
We can make love a serious crime
I said, we can make love a serious crime

I'm the con man on the corner
You're the kid with X-ray eyes
I'm coming up fast, get out, get out of my way
'It's just infatuation'
You keep thinking to yourself
Your mind's made up there's nothing I can I say

Once I dreamt about the future
Till I woke up in the past
And as concepts go, that's way, way over my head
Just take a look around you
And then tell me what you find
It reminds me of a book that I once read
Or was it something someone else had said?

So if you seek, you'll find
Feel like I've been in love since the end of time
So you better get a move on fast
Or we'll all be left behind
We could make love a serious crime
I said, we can make love a serious crime

So if you seek, you'll find
Feel like I've been in love since the end of time
So you'd better get a move on fast
Or we'll all be left behind
We can make love a serious crime
I said, we can make love a serious crime

A serious crime
A serious crime
A serious crime

Sixteen

You know I don't like dancin'
An' I don't like to bop
Too much movement's exertion
Makes me wish I could drop
Dro', dro', dro', dro', dro', dro', drop

An' I don't like french kissin'
'Cos you swallow my tongue
And you think that you're oh so very old
You only want me 'cos you think I'm so young
Yo', yo', yo', yo', yo', yo', young

All right
Ok
No way

An' I wish I was sixteen again
Then things would be such fun
All the things I'd do would be the same
But they're much more fun
Than when you're twenty wo', wo', wo', wo', wo,' one

All right
Ok
No way

An' I hate modern music
Disco boogie pop
They go on an' on an' on an' on an' on
How I wish they would stop

Sixteen Again

Feeling like I'm almost sixteen again
Layin' round doing nothing like all my friends
Play it cool don't get angry count up to ten
Just like I was sixteen again

No one gets the lowdown right from the start
Everybody gets the showdown right from the heart
But that's all that's on the menu and life's à la carte
I don't know

Things in life are not played for keeps
If it makes you happy it'll make you weep
And if you want some more practical advice
If you can't think once then don't think twice
'Cos things won't seem so nice
You'll wish you were sixteen again
Oh no

Feeling rather strange when you're sixteen again
Things don't seem the same the past is so plain
This future is our future this time's not a game
The time you're sixteen again

Always on your own when there's nobody else
Asking myself 'would I be someone else?'
But after all life's only death's recompense
I don't know

Things in life are not played for keeps
If it makes you happy it'll make you weep
And if you want some more practical advice
If you can't think once then don't think twice
'Cos things won't seem so nice
You'll wish you were sixteen again
Oh no

Look at me here I am for your eyes
Mirrored proof of what you recognize
I know I never will feel quite like you
And I know that you won't treat me right till I do
But at least we'll know it's true
That I'm sixteen again
Oh no

Feeling like I'm almost sixteen again
Lazin' round doing nothing like all my friends
Play it cool don't get angry count up to ten
Just like I was sixteen again

Always on your own when there's nobody else
Asking myself 'would I be someone else?'
But after all life's only death's recompense
I don't know

Look at me here I am for your eyes
Mirrored proof of love's suicide
I know I never will feel quite like you
And I know that you won't treat me right till I do
But at least we'll know it's true
That I'm sixteen again
Oh no

Sixteen again
Sixteen again

Smile

If I never ever, ever get to see you again
Remember it was you that made me smile
You satisfy the need you created
Not for the first time could be for real

And in times of desperation when I needed a friend
Remember it was you that made it all worthwhile
I sometimes try to fake hesitation
Not for the first time I've started to feel

Straight, straight through my heart those arrows fly
Straight, straight through my heart now that's no lie

I don't want to play the innocent you know me too well
You still keep me wondering but I don't know why
You satisfy the need you created
And for the first time I feel so real

Straight, straight through my heart those arrows fly
Straight, straight through my heart and that's no lie

Wait, wait for me please don't pass me by
If this world's without you I'd surely die
I'm in the middle of a love without an end
Reality too easy to comprehend

Straight, straight through my heart those arrows fly
Straight, straight through my heart and that's no lie

Wait, wait for me please don't pass me by
If this world's without you I'd surely die
I'm in the middle of a love without an end
Reality too easy to comprehend

Kono yono nani yori ichiban daisuki yo
Remember it was you that made me smile

Sneaky

I sense your indecision
You won't make up your mind
You're in the dark no light to guide each turn
It matters what I say and do
And truth's the light to guide you through
Adversity's the lessons we must learn

Oh, sneaky, sneaky
Will you ever have the time?

I'm with you in my dreaming
I just want you to stay
Don't take away my very heart and soul
There's no real need to say goodbye
Because you are the reason why
And staying on the path's the only goal

Oh, sneaky, sneaky
You never have the time to give all your attention to me
Oh, sneaky, sneaky
Will you ever have the time?

I sense your indecision
You won't make up your mind
You're in the dark no light to guide each turn
It matters what I say and do
And truth's the light to guide you through
Adversities, the lessons we must learn

Oh, sneaky, sneaky
You never have the time to give all your attention to me
Oh, sneaky, sneaky
Will you ever have the time?

Oh, sneaky, sneaky
You never have the time to give all your attention to me
Oh, sneaky, sneaky
Will you ever have the time?

Oh, sneaky, sneaky

Some Kinda Wonderful

The way you are to me
I must be blind I didn't see
I can't believe that this could happen with you
All my wildest dreams
Had fallen apart at the seams
But at the moment I hope this one is true

Right there in the palm of my hand
Tell me how could I have been such a fool?
I'm not gonna make no demands on you
'Cos you're some kinda wonderful

I took a double take
And gave myself an even break
You know I never thought of you in that way
But with a love so strong
I can't see what we do is wrong
I just don't care whatever people might say

Right there in the palm of my hand
Tell me how could I have been such a fool?
I'm not gonna make no demands on you
'Cos you're some kinda wonderful

Right there in the palm of my hand
Tell me how could I have been such a fool?
I'm not gonna make no demands on you
'Cos you're some kinda wonderful

The way I feel about you
I find hard to explain
I hear a voice is it my name you're calling

It couldn't come a minute too soon
'Cos you're some kinda wonderful
I'm up there with the Man in the Moon
'Cos you're some kinda wonderful
I'm not gonna make no demands on you
'Cos you're some kinda wonderful
I'm not gonna make no demands on you
'Cos you're some kinda wonderful

Something's Gone Wrong Again

Tried to find my sock
No good it's lost
Something's gone wrong again
Need a shave
Cut myself need a new blade
Something's gone wrong again
And again and again and again, again and
Something's gone wrong again
Something's gone wrong again

Tried to fry an egg
Broke the yolk no joke
Something's gone wrong again
Look at my watch just to tell the time
But the hand's come off mine
Something's gone wrong again
Something's gone wrong again
And again and again and again, again and
Something's gone wrong again
Something's gone wrong again

Nothing ever happens to people like us
'Cept we miss the bus
Something goes wrong again
Need a smoke use my last 50p
But the machine is broke
Something's gone wrong again
Something goes wrong again
And again and again and again, again and
Something goes wrong again
Something goes wrong again

Something goes wrong again
And again and again and again, again and
Something goes wrong again

Something goes wrong again

Nothing ever happens to people like us
'Cept we miss the bus
Something goes wrong again
Need a smoke use my last 50p
But the machine is broke
Something goes wrong again
Something goes wrong again
And again and again and again, again and
Something goes wrong again
Something goes wrong again

I turn up early in time for our date
But then you turn up late
Something goes wrong again
Need a drink go to the pub
But the bugger's shut
Something goes wrong again
Something goes wrong again
And again and again and again, again and
Something goes wrong again
Ah, something goes wrong again
Something goes wrong again
Something goes wrong again

Soul On A Rock

This desolation sweeping over me
I find hard to disguise
The contradiction what I want and what I see
Has led to darkening skies
And I don't know if you're just deceiving me
And I just hope that you're not deceiving me

I often wonder are there secrets that you've kept
With some other guy?
Some consolation it hasn't happened yet
Or was that just a lie?
And I just hope that you're not deceiving me
And I don't know if you're just deceiving me

My soul on a rock
I know what I feel
My soul on a rock
It hurts 'cause it's real
My soul on a rock
I wanna believe

I often wonder are there secrets that you've kept
With that other guy?
Some consolation it hasn't happened yet
Or is that just a lie?
And I just hope that you're not deceiving me
My soul on a rock
I know what I feel
My soul on a rock
It hurts 'cause it's real
My soul on a rock
I wanna believe

My soul on a rock
I know what I feel
My soul on a rock

It hurts 'cos it's real
My soul on a rock
I wanna believe
And I just hope that you're not deceiving me

My soul on a rock
I know what I feel
My soul on a rock
It hurts 'cause it's real
My soul on a rock
I wanna believe
And I just hope that you're not deceiving me

My soul on a rock
I know what I feel
My soul on a rock
It hurts 'cause it's real
My soul on a rock
I wanna believe

Strange Thing

Strange thing happened one day
Someone thought they heard someone say
'Gotta face new directions'
'Get new expectations'
Strange thing happened one day
Someone thought they heard someone say
'Get rid of complications'
'Free yourself from frustrations'
Gotta control depression
Gotta control this depression

Strange thing happened today
I thought I heard somebody say
'Gotta face new directions'
'Get new expectations'
Strange thing happened today
I thought I heard somebody say
'Get rid of complications'
'Free yourself from frustrations'
Gotta control depression
Gotta control this depression

Strange things will happen one day
You think you hear somebody say
'Gotta face new directions'
'Get new expectations'
Strange thing will happen one day
You think you hear somebody say
'Get rid of complications'
'Free yourself from your frustrations'
Gotta control depression
Gotta, gotta control this depression

Telephone Operator

Telephone Operator
Why can't I see you later?
Telephone Operator
Why can't I see you later?
Tell me is it wine
That makes things so fine
Or is it 'cos you're mine?

Telephone Operator
You're my aural stimulator
Telephone Operator
N'est-ce pas la raison d'être
Tell me is it love
That I feel because
You're all I'm thinking of?

Telephone Operator
Phone you up an hour later
Telephone Operator
Phoned you up an hour later
Tell me is it love
That I'm in because
I'm only thinking of you?

They're Coming For You

Too much thinking is a dangerous thing
You left me standing waiting on my own
All I want is a passionate relationship
You just wanna stay at home
To save money gotta pay the price
'Cos nothing never ever's really free

'Stay tuned for details', was all I heard him say
I wonder what I should try and do?
The phones are tapped and the television's looking at me
So how on earth can I get through?
Hide in a corner, wait till it's all over
Hold my breath until I turn blue

They're coming for you
They're coming for you
You say you care but I don't believe you do
Even though I know how hard you try
Didn't I tell you long ago?
Didn't I tell you long ago?

Think of tomorrow as the only time we have
Trapped between Heaven and the sea
And everything that happens to you
I'm sure will happen to me
I only hope that I'm not in
When they come knocking at your door

'Stay tuned for details', was all I heard him say
I wonder what I should try and do
The phones are tapped and the television's looking at me
So how on earth can I get through
Hide in the corner, wait till it's all over
Hold my breath until I turn blue

They're coming for you
They're coming for you
You say you care but I don't believe you do
Even though I know how hard you try
Didn't I tell you long ago?
Didn't I tell you long ago?

Think of tomorrow as the only time we have
Trapped between Heaven and the sea
And everything that happens to you
I'm sure will happen to me
I only hope that I'm not in
When they come knocking at your door

They're coming for you
They're coming for you
You say you care but I don't believe you do
Even though I know how hard you try
Didn't I tell you long ago?
Didn't I tell you long ago?

They're coming for you
They're coming for you
You say you care but I don't believe you do
Even though I know how hard you try
Didn't I tell you long ago?
Didn't I tell you long ago?

The Way

It happens right before your eyes
But still it takes you by surprise
You sit and watch it on TV
I even saw it on a documentary
Ignorance kills, it's a clash of wills
No panacea's gonna cure your ills
I'm feeling kind of indiscreet
Patience is bitter, its fruit is so sweet

So keep a straight face and look me in my eye
And say you wouldn't take this from any other guy
I haven't got the time to spare
The way you are's not the way you were

Uninspired, I'm sick and tired
You're hyperactive, totally wired
Stay with me and we could have such fun
After all, we're answerable to no one
Cyberporn from dusk till dawn
Nowhere to hide from the suicide bomb
Outside forces come inside to play
You wouldn't even treat a dog that way

So keep a straight face and look me in my eye
And say you wouldn't take this from any other guy
Besieging castles in the air
The way you are's not the way you were
The way you are's not the way you were
The way you are's not the way you were
The way you are's not the way you were

So keep a straight face and look me in my eye
And say you wouldn't get this from any other guy
I haven't got the time to spare
The way you are's not the way you were

So keep a straight face and look me in my eye
And say you wouldn't take this from any other guy
Besieging castles in the air
The way you are's not the way you were
The way you are's not the way you were
The way you are's not the way you were
The way you are's not the way you were

Thunder Of Hearts

Tell me why you look the other way
I've been tired of being blind
From staring at the sun
No cause for celebration tonight

Ok, right you win
But always remember
Don't say you've not heard
When you die you're dead for ever

Yes, sometimes even monkeys fall from trees
The die is cast your mind's made up
We're going on our way
In my life this is happening to me

You live what you learn
I'll beg steal or borrow
The thunder of hearts
Will echo tomorrow

Ok, right you win
But always remember
I've said you've not heard
When you die you're dead for ever

It's not that much of a mystery
I need things sorta how they ought to be
And me down here on bended knee
Such sympathy is too much to ignore

I know a thing or two
Well, more than three
I want it to be perfect
What a wish should be
No chance of celebration tonight

You live what you learn
I'd beg steal or borrow
The thunder of hearts will echo tomorrow
Ok, right you win
But always remember
I've said now you've heard
When you die you're dead for ever
Forever

Totally From The Heart

You want more
More than I can deliver
I love you
More than you could ever know now
Made it plain from the start
Totally from the heart

I'm to you
Like the mountain to Muhammad
But these roles
Could be juxtaposed
It's up to you now
Made it plain from the start
Totally from the heart

Totally from the heart

Can't you hear a word I'm sayin'?
Every night I lie here prayin'
I'm so scared
I'm too scared of being alone
So lonely, lonely, lonely
Till the next time

Look at me
While I try to think about you
Look at me
While I try to think about you

Made it plain from the start
Totally from the heart

Totally from the heart

Can't you hear a word I'm sayin'?
Every night I lie here prayin'

I'm so scared
I'm too scared of being alone
So lonely, lonely, lonely, lonely, lonely
Lonely, lonely, lonely
Till the next time

From now on
Is the time for becoming
One by one
We can take control
I'm telling you now
Make it plain from the start
Totally from the heart

You want more
More than I can deliver
I love you
More than you could ever know
I'm to you
Like the mountain to Muhammad
But these roles
Could be juxtaposed

Make it plain from the start

TTT

Turn the television on
You've been reading too long
Turn your radios on
And I'll sing you a song

Let's get back to basics
I know just what you need
I'm talented by the way you feel
Flattery's a deed of attraction
It seems you're changing direction to me

Turn the television on
You've been reading too long
Turn your stereo on
And I'll sing you a song

Charity's a good investment
What hard times we're living through
Thinking of us face to face like this
So this is what destiny feels like
Adapt, improvise, overcome

Turn the television on
You've been reading too long
Turn the radios on
Nothing else is going on

Trade test transmission
Turn the television on
Nothing else is going on

Turn the television on
You've been reading too long
Turn your radios on
I will sing you my song

Trade test transmission
Turn the television on
Nothing else is going on

Trade test transmission
Turn the television on
Nothing else is going on
Turn me on
Turn me on

Twilight

Watching the twilight
I saw it flicker
Think that I might as well give up and go
On the horizon
Are distant reminders
Twilight is the only love I know

Shadows dissolving
No good me trying
I always find it hard to leave and let go
I knew that you loved me
Guess I was mistaken
Twilight is the only love I know

Under The Sun

I never meant to drive you away
I really want you to stay
I feel you're being unkind
When you say I'm a waste of time
But I can't get you out of my mind

Been the same since long ago
Give and take
Takes two you know
Only goes to show
There's nothing new under the sun

And when I feel on a roll
You open up my soul
Is it or isn't it me?
Was I so blind that I just couldn't see?
I'm tired of this ambiguity

Been the same since long ago
Give and take
Takes two you know?
Only goes to show
There's nothing new under the sun

All uphill
Feelings low
Such a little so and so
Only goes to show
There's nothing new under the sun

Why on earth can I never win?
Why has fate such a mocking grin?
Is it or isn't it me?
Was I so blind that I just couldn't see?
I'm tired of this ambiguity

Why on earth can I never win?
Why has fate such a mocking grin?
I feel you're being unkind
When you say I'm a waste of time
But I can't get you out of my mind

Been the same since long ago
Give and take
Takes two you know?
Only goes to show
There's nothing new under the sun

All uphill
Feelings low
Such a little so and so
Only goes to show
There's nothing new under the sun
Only goes to show
There's nothing new under the sun
New under the sun

Useless

Life's full of disappointments
Wonder where the good times went
Craving for recognition
Rather than accomplishment
Nobody cares what your name is
And it's gonna stay that way
Everything is off the record
Face it there's nothing to say
Life's only temporary
And then you fuckin' die

It's a useless situation
Can't you see that I'm
Between patience and persuasion
Every single time?

Mingling amongst the masses
That much would be enough
You used to be my rival
Quit when the going gets rough
I never witnessed the moment
When all you ever wanted was me
Understand now the penny's dropped
Pissed off bunny not happy
Don't wanna think about it
It makes me fuckin' mad

It's a useless situation
Can't you see that I'm
Between patience and persuasion
Every single time?
It's a useless situation
Can't you see that I'm
Between patience and persuasion
Every single time?

I never witnessed the moment
When all you ever wanted was me
Understand now the penny drops
Pissed off bunny not happy
Life's only temporary
And then you fuckin' die

It's a useless situation
Can't you see that I'm
Between patience and persuasion
Every single time?
It's a useless situation
Can't you see that I'm
Between patience and persuasion
Every single time?

Virtually Real

You fill your life with social media
Lolcats, confessions of shiba
Flash mobs gatecrash your party
Your views just retweets of the twitterati

Profile updated
It's complicated
So tell me how do you feel?
Virtually real

I see the world full of hidden dangers
Hackers, trolls
Anonymous strangers
Why waste your time liking and sharing
Instead of with me
Loving and caring?

Profile updated
It's complicated
So tell me how do you feel?
Virtually real

Waiting For Love

Waiting for love
You keep me waiting for love

Sometimes I understand more than I feel
It keeps me in command of what is real
Waiting for love
You keep me waiting for love

I often wonder what I came here for
But I know it's something that I can't ignore
Waiting for love
You keep me waiting for love

There's no need in your disguise
For I've seen the colour of your eyes

Waiting for love
You keep me waiting for love

There's no need in this disguise
For I've seen the passion in your eyes

All I need is respect
All I want is a love that is real
Is that too much to expect?
Am I being unreasonable?
All I need is a friend
But more than a friend
But I tend to suspect
I haven't a chance of getting romance
But I guess that it'll make no difference to me

Waiting for love
You keep me waiting for love
You keep me waiting for love
You keep me waiting for love

What Do I Get?

I just want a lover
Like any other
What do I get?
I only want a friend
Who will stay to the end
What do I get?

What do I get?
Oh, oh
What do I get ?
What do I get?
Oh, oh
What do I get?

I'm in distress
I need a caress
What do I get?
I'm not on the make
I just need a break
What do I get?

What do I get?
Oh, oh
What do I get?
What do I get?
Oh, oh
What do I get?

I only get sleepless nights
Alone here in my half-empty bed
For you things seem to turn out right
I wish they'd only happen to me instead

What do I get?
Oh, oh
What do I get?
What do I get?
Oh, oh
What do I get?

I only get sleepless nights
Alone here in my half-empty bed
For you things seem to turn out right
I wish they'd only happen to me instead

What do I get?
Oh, oh
What do I get?
What do I get?
Oh, oh
What do I get?

I just want a lover
Like any other
What do I get?
I only want a friend
Who will love to the end
What do I get?

What do I get?
Oh, oh
What do I get?
What do I get?
Oh, oh
What do I get?

Well let me tell you now

I get no love
I get no sleep at nights
I get nothing that's nice
I get nothing at all
At all, at all, at all
At all, at all, at all
'Cos I don't get you

What Do You Know?

Everything happens
Don't look for patterns
You only perceive what you believe
You need only believe to believe

A map of illusion
Of this land of confusion
I saw the boy clad in leather
For ever and ever and ever

What do you know?
What do you know?
What do you know?
What do you know?
What do you know?

There's no turning back now
I'm under attack now
I don't need a mirror to see
Just what has happened to me

There's no contradiction
Between fact and fiction
I saw the skies open
And I heard the word spoken

What do you know?
What do you know?
What do you know?
What do you know?
What do you know?

What do you know?
What do you know?
What do you know?

What do you know?
What do you know?

Everything happens
Don't look for patterns
You only perceive what you believe
You need only believe and you'll believe

A map of illusion
Of this land of confusion
I see a boy clad in leather
For ever and ever and ever

There's no turning back now
I'm under attack now
I see the skies are open
And I hear the word spoken

You only perceive what you believe
You need only believe to believe

What do you know?
What do you know?
What do you know?
What do you know?
What do you know?
What do you know?
What do you know?

What Was Heaven?

I can't run to the light
It's you that I need
I could cut myself with a knife
For you babe and bleed

What was Heaven without you babe?
Now everything is complete
I sometimes wish it's a novel
And I'd see you in the street

All the day is the night
But somehow I just can't sleep
Somehow though it don't seem right
I had you but love didn't keep

What was Heaven without you babe?
Now everything is complete
I sometimes wish it's a novel
And I'd see you in the street

Sometimes I hear your voice
Echoing it makes me cry
I don't seem to have the choice
I want you but I don't wanna die

What was Heaven without you babe?
Now everything is complete
I sometimes wish it's a novel
And I'd see you in the street

What You Mean To Me

There's a road ahead
Past a stormy sea
There I will return
That's just what you mean to me

Neath a darkening sky
Where no soul is free
There my lover lies
That's just what you mean to me
Just exactly what you mean to me
What you mean to me
Just exactly what you mean to me

Have no need for fate
I've got destiny
All things come to pass
That's just what you mean to me
Just exactly what you mean to me
What you mean to me
Just exactly what you mean to me

I contemplate every moment
Let's make history
Tired of sharing my loneliness alone
That's just what you mean to me
Just exactly what you mean to me

Someday soon you'll know
One day soon you'll see
Why I sing this song
That's just what you mean to me
Just exactly what you mean to me
What you mean to me
Just exactly what you mean to me

This whole crazy world
Don't amount to more than a hill of beans
Tired of sharing my loneliness alone
I wanna live my dreams
I contemplate every moment
Let's make history
It's time now to be the future
That's just what you mean to me
Just exactly what you mean to me
What you mean to me
Just exactly what you mean to me

It's time now to be the future
Let's make history

Who'll Help Me To Forget?

Now that your love's not real
You leave me lying on my own
I find it kinda rich you know
When something goes to nothing
Then again I guess I should've known

Was it all a waste of time
A game I'm not supposed to win?
No matter what I try
It seems to make no difference
I'll just have to start all over again

I'm trying oh so hard to be a man about it
I'd like to see your point of view
But you always refuse to even talk about it
This isn't just a phase I'm going through

Now you've made up your mind
Please tell me why is life so cruel?
While you act the Lear of love
You have me typecast as the fool
But there is a question
That's still unanswered yet
I said who'll help me to forget?

Was it all a waste of time
A game I'm not supposed to win?
No matter what I try
It seems to make no difference
I'll just have to start all over again

I'm trying oh so hard to be a man about it
I'd like to see your point of view
But you always refuse to even talk about it
This isn't just a phase I'm going through

Now you've made up your mind
Please tell me why is life so cruel
While you act the Lear of love
You have me typecast as the fool
But there is a question
That's still unanswered yet
I said who'll help me to forget?
I said who'll help me to forget?

I'm trying oh so hard to be a man about it
I'd like to see your point of view
But you always refuse to even talk about it
This isn't just a phase I'm going through

Now you've made up your mind
Please tell me why is life so cruel?
While you act the Lear of love
You have me typecast as the fool
But there is a question
That's still unanswered yet
I said who'll help me to forget?

Now you've made up your mind
Please tell me why is life so cruel?
While you act the Lear of love
You have me cast down as the fool
But there is a question
That's still unanswered yet
I said who'll help me to forget?
I said who'll help me to forget?

Why Can't I Touch It?

Well it seems so real I can see it
And it seems so real I can feel it
And it seems so real I can taste it
And it seems so real I can hear it
So why can't I touch it?
So why can't I touch it?

Then it looks so real I can see it
And it feels so real I can feel it
And it tastes so real I can taste it
And it sounds so real I can hear it
So why can't I touch it?
So why can't I touch it?

Then it looks so real I can feel it
And it feels so real I can taste it
And it tastes so real I can hear it
And it sounds so real I can see it
So why can't I touch it?
So why can't I touch it?

Now it is so real I can see it
And it is so real I can feel it
And it is so real I can hear it
And it is so real I can be it
So why can't I touch it?
So why can't I touch it?

Why Compromise?

I'm not pretending so don't ask why
Your time is coming and that's no lie
You're the exception that proves the rule
From where I'm standing you're nobody's fool

I've been a bad boy
So do what you please
Talking of pleasure
Speak in Japanese
There's no good or evil
Only different degrees
Hope springs eternal
When you're down on your knees

You read the papers I watch TV
I'm tired of living in history
You've had your pleasure now here comes the pain
As sure as sunshine follows the rain

Under my direction
Let me see you blaspheme
Looking for a traitor
If you know what I mean
Overnight sensations
Just fade away
Nothing lasts forever
I don't care what you say

Immaculate conception
Here's a word to the wise
If there's no opposition
Why compromise?
There's no good or evil
Only different degrees
Hope springs eternal
When you're down on your knees

Let's put our hands together
And deal a pack of lies
We won't live forever
Why compromise?

Wish I Never Loved You

No matter what I try
Is no good for you
Everything that I say
Everything that I do
It's crystal clear now
That we're going nowhere
And that once was a dream
Has become this nightmare
Wish I never loved you
But I just can't let go

Now I know how it feels
To have loved and lost
Because of pride
To be deserted
So that hurt is
All that's left inside
I'm ashamed
I've been blamed
So much I wanted to die
Tell me why, tell me why
Tell me why, tell me why

Wish I never loved you
But I just can't let go

Now I know how it feels
To have loved and lost
Because of pride
To be deserted
So that hurt is
All that's left inside

I'm ashamed
I've been blamed
So much I wanted to die
Tell me why, tell me why
Tell me why, tell me why
Tell me why, tell me why
Tell me why, tell me why

What makes me think
I mean nothing to you?
Everything that you say
Everything that you do
All your excuses
The lies you invent
Provide more than
A little discouragement
Wish I never loved you
But I just can't let go

Now I know how it feels
To have loved and lost
Because of pride
To be deserted
So that hurt is
All that's left inside
I'm ashamed
I've been blamed
So much I wanted to die
Tell me why, tell me why
Tell me why, tell me why
To be deserted
So that hurt is
All that's left inside
I'm ashamed
I've been blamed

So much I wanted to die

Tell me why, tell me why
Tell me why, tell me why
To be deserted
So that hurt is
All that's left inside
I'm ashamed
I've been blamed
So much I wanted to die
Tell me why, tell me why
Tell me why, tell me why
Tell me why, tell me why
Tell me why, tell me why
Tell me why, tell me why
Tell me why, tell me why
Tell me why, tell me why
Tell me why, tell me why

Without You

I'm running out of valuable time
Without you
Am I a victim of your serial crime
Or just a taboo?
You know that

Whenever we're together you just tear me apart
A filament of my illumination
Love that's never ever isn't really that smart
How could I be so blind?

Since you left me I live life day by day
Without you
And at the risk of sounding like a cliché
It's making me blue
You know that

Whenever we're together you just tear me apart
A filament of my illumination
Love that's never ever isn't really that smart
How could I be so blind?
I just can't get you out of my mind

Is that fear and loathing that I see shine through your eyes?
A sheep in wolf's clothing well it took me by surprise

Whenever we're together you just tear me apart
A filament of my illumination
Love that's never ever isn't really that smart
How could I be so blind?
I just can't get you out of my mind

I'm running out of valuable time
Without you
Am I a victim of your serial crime
Or just a taboo?
You know that

Whenever we're together you just tear me apart
A filament of my illumination
Love that's never ever isn't really that smart
How could I be so blind ?
I just can't get you out of my mind

Is that fear and loathing that I see shine through your eyes?
A sheep in wolf's clothing would have fell for your disguise
A sheep in wolf's clothing well it took me by surprise
How could I be so blind?
I just can't get you out of my mind
Out of my mind

Witness The Change

In my mind there are mirrors
Reflecting on the past
The shattered hopes and dreams of a future
That was never meant to last

Just turn around now
Tell me what you see
Look all around you
Is this how things could be?

Had enough of love never lasting
But now I know it never will
Hanging around on the off chance
Waiting for that certain thrill

Just turn around now
See what we have done
It's getting late now
The future has begun

Witness the change
Witness the change
Witness the change
Witness the change
Witness the change
Witness the change

Some kinds of love are magical mystical
I wonder how I'd feel
If ever I should be so enchanted
To get a taste of what is real

Just look around now
Tell me what you see

Look all around you
Is this how things could be?

I feel the sound of thunder and laughter
It's tearing me apart
I start to fade till all that's remaining is
The echo of my heart

Just look around you
See what we have done
It's getting late now
The future has begun

Witness the change
Witness the change
Witness the change
Witness the change
Witness the change
Witness the change
Witness the change
Witness the change
Witness the change
Witness the change
Witness the change
Witness the change

I have a feeling
And I know it will never die
Part of the answer
For asking the reason why
Out of the darkness
The bright light surrounding me
I am a part of
Everything I touch and see

I feel the sound of thunder and laughter
It's tearing me apart
I hope that you will remember
The echo of my heart

Witness the change
Witness the change
Witness the change
Witness the change
Witness the change
Witness the change
Witness the change
Witness the change
Witness the change
Witness the change
Witness the change
Witness the change
Witness the change
Witness the change
Witness the change
Witness the change
Witness the change
Witness the change

XL1

You talked about the weather
What could I say?
We're never seen together
We hide away

Didn't know what dreams were for
Didn't know what friends were for
Didn't know what love was for
You still don't know now
XL1

You had a secret passion
I had one too
You tend to follow fashion
Do what I do

Didn't know what dreams were for
Didn't know what friends were for
Didn't know what love was for
You still don't know now
XL1

You talked about the weather
What could I say?
We're never seen together
We hide away

Didn't know what dreams were for
Didn't know what friends were for
Didn't know what love was for
You still don't know now
XL1

Didn't know what dreams were for
Didn't know what friends were for
Didn't know what love was for
You still don't know now
XL1

Yesterday's Not Here

Looking back on life is such a retrospective thing
Hoping for some nice advice that only you could bring
But you came as in a storm
When the woolly dreams were shorn off my back
Suffer cold reality's sting

All my life that I remember was a drag
Even though it wasn't so good it was all that I'd had
Now I've seen it slip away and tomorrow's just another day
To find relief from feeling sad

Yesterday's not here no more
It's gone for good and I'm glad 'cos it made me sore
All the things that might have been
Are seen by me as regrets that my memory stores

All my life that I remember was a drag
Even though it wasn't so good it was all that I'd had
Now I've seen it slip away and tomorrow's just another day
To find relief from feeling sad

Yesterday's not here no more
It's gone for good and I'm glad 'cos it made me sore
All the things that might have been
Are seen by me as regrets that my memory stores

But from all my time the things I have seen
Have I seen you or have I been
A mirror of what you wanted to be?
Just almost like you were to me
To me, to me, to me

Yesterday's not here no more
It's gone for good and I'm glad 'cos it made me sore
All the things that might have been
Are seen by me as regrets that my memory stores

Yesterday's not here no more
Oh, yesterday's not here no more
Oh, yesterday's not here no more
Oh, yesterday's not here no more
Oh, yesterday's not here no more

You And I

You and I will never change
Though we're different we'll remain the same
Love's devoid of reason anyway
Finder's keepers so they say
What I grasp at only fades away
Love's devoid of reason anyway

I heard something you know I
Know that it's true
You know it makes no difference
What you try to do
You know that
Love will always take you by surprise
I feel something special
But I just don't know why

You and I could have such fun
The evening's over the party's just begun
Love dissolves all reason anyway
In the space between the lines
There's the truth that we'd all like to find
What's the point of reason anyway?

I heard something you know I
Know that it's true
You know it makes no difference
What you try to do
You know that
Love will always take you by surprise
I feel something special
But I just don't know why

In point of fact
You know it's plain to see
I've got a real thing going here

Not fantasy

You know that
I won't treat you like those other guys
As time is my witness
I don't have the need for alibis

You and I will never change
Though we're different we'll remain the same
Love's devoid of reason anyway
Finder's keepers so they say
What I grasp at only fades away
What's the point of reason anyway?

You Can't Take That Away

You're so different
You remind me a lot of myself
A few years ago maybe
No regrets
I've often wondered what I'd do
If I had my time again

Daydreaming's easy
But living life is strictly one way
No turning back
No map
We all go astray
Still I guess I'm telling you something
That you could testify

As time passes by
I still don't know why
You've taken every thing from me but love

I tried to reason with you
But you had made up your mind
We argued in whispers
If I live till I die
I never want to go to hell again

The phases of the moon
The seasons the years won't erase
The silent echo of your dream in my heart
My eyes are burning
Tears are running down my cheeks
As I start to cry

As time passes by

I still don't know why
You've taken every thing from me but love
As time passes by
I still don't know why
You've taken every thing from me but love

Oh, you can't take that away from me
Oh, no you can't take that away from me
There is no future and the past is all lies
But with each heartbeat another part of me dies
You can't take that away from me

As time passes by
I still don't know why
You've taken every thing from me but love
As time passes by
I still don't know why
You've taken every thing from me but love

Oh, you can't take that away from me
Oh, no you can't take that away from me
There is no future and the past is all lies
But with each heartbeat another part of me dies
Oh, you can't take that away from me
Oh, no you can't take that away from me
Oh, no you can't take that away from me
Oh, no you can't take that away from me
Oh, no you can't take that away from me

You Know Better Than I Know

Understanding don't come easy
Love's a state of mind
Trying hard just to make it perfect
Tryna make life rhyme
Questions only lead to questions
Round and round they spin
There's no need to make excuses for
The shape that you're in

You know better than I know
That we'll always feel the same
And you know better than I know
So there's no need to explain

And so it makes no difference
I guess we'll never win
We'll just have to pick ourselves up
And start all over again

I'm consumed by a passion burning
So deep inside
I know that I'll always love you
I couldn't even leave you if I tried
Need you more than ever
You make me complete
You supply me with the danger that
Makes life so sweet

You know better than I know
That we'll always feel the same
And you know better than I know
So there's no need to explain

And if it makes no difference
I guess we'll never win
We'll just have to pick ourselves up
And start all over again

Lying in the darkness
And I just can't get to sleep
Sorting out my thoughts
But I don't know which are the right ones to keep
Thinking of the countries
Where there's nothing left to eat
Counting the starving millions by the thousand
I fall asleep

And if it makes no difference
I guess we'll never win
We'll just have to pick ourselves up
And start all over again

Understanding don't come easy
Love's a state of mine
I know that I'll always love you
I couldn't even leave you if I tried
Need you more than ever
Where do I begin?
I've no need to make excuses for
The state that I'm in

You know better than I know
That we'll always feel the same
And you know better than I know
So there's no need to explain

And if it makes no difference
I guess we'll never win
We'll just have to pick ourselves up
And start all over again
Start all over again
Start all over again

You know better than I know
You know better than I know
You know better than I know
You know better than I know

You Say You Don't Love Me

You say you don't love me
Well that's all right with me
'Cos I'm in love with you
And I wouldn't want you doing things
You don't want to do
Oh, you know I've always wanted you
To be in love with me
And it took so long to realise
The way things have to be
I wanted to live in a dream
That couldn't be real
And I'm starting to understand now
The way that you feel
You say you don't
You say you don't

You say you don't love me
Well that's all right with me
'Cos I have got the time
To wait in case someday
You maybe change your mind
I've decided not to make
The same mistakes this time around
As I'm tired of having heartaches
I've been thinking and I've found
I don't want to live in a dream
I want something real
And I think I understand now
The way that you feel
You say you don't
You say you don't
You say you don't

You say you don't
You say you don't

You say you don't love me
Well that's all right with me
I'm not in love with you
I just want us to do the things
We both want to do
Though I've got this special feelin'
I'd be wrong to call it love
For the word entails a few things
That I would be well rid of
I've no need to live in a dream
It's finally real
And I hope you now understand
This feeling I feel
You say you don't
You say you don't
You say you don't love me
You say you don't love me
You say you don't love me
Mmm

Your Love

Whenever I feel like this
I notice that you are near to me
I struggle but can't resist
I can't fight my destiny
I put my world in your hands
Casting caution to the wind
I hope that you'll understand
'Cos here I go again

Your love
So warm inside me
Your love
Please don't deny me
Your love

They say it's a passing phase
And that it might not last
I guess that I can't complain
If the good times are gone too fast

Your love
So warm inside me
Your love
Please don't deny me
Your love's as precious as the desert rain
Your love
Your love makes the whole world seem right again
Your love

Your love
So warm inside me
Your love
Please don't deny me
Your love's as precious as the desert rain

Your love
Your love makes the whole world seem right again
Your love

They say it's a passing phase
And that it might not last
But when my life is through
The thought of you will be my last

Your love
So warm inside me
Your love
Please don't deny me
Your love's as precious as the desert rain
Your love
Your love makes the whole world seem right again
Your love
So deep inside me
Your love
Please don't deny me
Your love

369

I guess it's not my lucky day today
Oh well
You've been good to me
You make me feel so happy
Can't believe that I deserve it though

Love's more than the silly games you play
Oh no
Play it casually
No need to get a sweat on
At least not at the moment so

369 all the time
What's the meaning in the number?
Somebody tell me
369 through my mind
All I'm getting is a number
Somebody help me
Please

Take this bitter cup away from me
Oh, oh
It takes two you know
So if you're feeling lonely
Why not start a conversation? No, no

Another bitter twist of irony
Ho ho
Not that easily
My heart is on the warpath
I don't need a reservation

369 all the time
What's the meaning in the number?
Somebody tell me
369 through my mind

All I'm getting is a number
Somebody tell me

369 so sublime
All I'm getting is a number
Somebody tell me
369 for the sixth time
What's this with that number?
Somebody help me

Now that you know you have no one
But yourself to blame
No matter which way you look at it
It still looks the same

I guess it's not my lucky day today
Oh well
You've been good to me
You make me feel so happy
Can't believe that I deserve it though

Discography

First published in 2018 by
Eyewear Publishing Ltd
Suite 333, 19–21 Crawford Street
Marylebone
London W1H 1PJ

Book and cover design by @MalcolmGarrett
Proofreading of lyrics by Peter Hough and Todd Swift
Cover image after sleeve design for Buzzcocks'
'Ever Fallen In Love (With Someone You Shouldn't've)',
after Marcel Duchamp ('Fluttering Hearts' 1936)

Printed in England by
TJ International Ltd, Padstow, Cornwall

www.eyewearpublishing.com
www.buzzcocks.com

ISBN 978-1-912477-15-9